American Justice 2015

American Justice 2015

The Dramatic Tenth Term of the Roberts Court

Steven V. Mazie

PENN

UNIVERSITY OF PENNSYLVANIA PRESS

PHILADELPHIA

Published by
University of Pennsylvania Press
Philadelphia, Pennsylvania 19104-4112

www.upenn.edu/pennpress
Printed in the United States of America

A Cataloging-in-Publication record is available
from the Library of Congress

Cover design by John Hubbard

ISBN 978-0-8122-4806-7 hardcover
ISBN 978-0-8122-9227-5 ebook

For My Family

Contents

Preface

Two-thirds of Americans, according to a 2012 survey, cannot name a single Supreme Court justice. Only 1 percent can name all nine. This surely owes something to the fact that the justices banish television cameras from their courtroom and deliberate in secret. But every June, when the justices wrap up their work before taking a summer vacation, a few particularly consequential decisions capture the interest of a broad swath of Americans.

In 2015, as both the month of June and the Supreme Court's term wound to a close, everyone's ears bent toward Washington, DC, to hear how the justices would rule on two of the most contentious political issues of recent memory: the Affordable Care Act, also known as Obamacare, and same-sex marriage. Both matters proved to be just as divisive on the bench as they are among the public. By a 6–3 margin, the justices rebuffed a technical challenge to the Affordable Care Act that would have caused eight million Americans to lose their newly won health insurance. And by a razor's-edge vote of 5–4, they recognized a constitutional right for gay and lesbian couples to wed nationwide.

The liberal victories in these two cases, *King v. Burwell* and *Obergefell v. Hodges,* were the headliners of "the best term for the left in at least a quarter century," in the words of Tom Goldstein, Supreme Court litigator and publisher of SCOTUSblog, the online mecca of Supreme Court–related information and analysis. But they were hardly the only left-leaning decisions of note. The justices also turned back a challenge that would have made it much harder to prove racial discrimination under the Fair Housing Act and permitted voters in Arizona to keep their Republican-dominated legislature out of the business of drawing electoral districts in the state. The court also handed religious-rights wins to American Muslims in two separate cases and expanded the rights of pregnant women in the workplace. There were rulings to cheer conservatives as well. Most notably, the justices permitted Oklahoma to use a controversial lethal-injection drug when executing criminals and reined in the power of the Environmental Protection Agency to regulate power plants.

The politics of the highest-profile rulings were not lost on the public. A Gallup poll measuring Americans' support for the court taken in July 2015 showed stark partisan divisions. Seventy-six percent of Democrats said they approved of the work the high court was doing, while only 18 percent of Republicans gave the justices a vote of confidence. The court's overall approval rating of 49 percent (just beating out President Obama, whose July rating was 45 percent), is down significantly from a high mark of 80 percent in the 1990s. But it is triple that of Congress, which is still the most maligned branch of the federal government.

Every year, the justices convene on the first Monday of October to begin their work. Between October 6, 2014, and June 29, 2015—the period known as October Term 2014 (or OT 2014 for short)—they held hearings and issued rulings in sixty-six cases. (Another eight cases were "summary reversals," which means the lower court's decision was overturned without written briefs or oral arguments.) *American Justice 2015* dives into the people, principles, and arguments at the heart of the fourteen most significant cases of Chief Justice John Roberts's tenth year at the helm. It aims to lay out the details of OT 2014 in clear, accessible terms and conveys the drama behind, and beyond, the big cases.

My editors at *The Economist*, where I am the Supreme Court correspondent, admonish me to make my coverage of the justices accessible to the educated layman in Bangalore or Bangkok. As a publication that covers the world and is read in more than two hundred countries, *The Economist* is no place for gratuitous dives into abstract legal doctrine, and it is a welcome challenge to translate jurisprudential jargon into something approximating the English language. In writing this book, I have imported that sensibility with an eye to edifying anyone with an interest in the Supreme Court. At the same time, having more than forty thousand words to play with (rather than my usual allotment of six hundred or so for a print piece) has liberated me to expand on the stories behind the cases and to offer a fuller account of the arguments driving them and the impact the rulings are likely to have.

I owe much to many people for making this book possible. Damon Linker, my editor at the University of Pennsylvania Press, suggested the project in December and helped greatly at the framing stage and throughout the process. Many thanks to him and to the Penn Press staff for producing this book so speedily and professionally. Over the past couple of years, I have learned much from a number of fantastically friendly and talented Supreme Court journalists—Lyle Denniston of SCOTUSblog, Adam Liptak of the *New York Times,* Dahlia Lithwick of *Slate,* Kenneth Jost of *CQ Press* and, most of all, the gregarious Garrett Epps of *The Atlantic.* They have welcomed me to the press gallery at the court and shown me the ropes of covering an oral argument. Garrett also offered helpful advice on my initial proposal for this book. I'd like to thank Patricia McCabe Estrada and Annie Stone in the Supreme Court's Public Information Office for finding room for me in the press gallery and for their cheerful guidance.

Exchanges with a number of people—Georgia State University law professor Eric Segall, high school debate partner and former Supreme Court litigator Matthew Shors, *New York Times* columnist and Yale law professor Linda Greenhouse, former Supreme Court clerk and college friend Robert Gordon, and Don Herzog, my dissertation advisor at the University of Michigan—all provoked me to think differently about cases and ideas discussed in this book.

Amy Howe at SCOTUSblog has been a constant source of insight and advice, not to mention infectious excitement about the drama that transpires at 1 First Street, Northeast. I'd like to thank Amy for reading and commenting on an early draft of my introduction. Other scholars and Supreme Court litigants were generous with their time in reviewing various parts of the manuscript. My thanks to Douglas Laycock of the University of Virginia School of Law for helpful suggestions on chapter 1. Orin Kerr, who teaches law at George Washington University, corrected gaps in my knowledge of the Fourth

Amendment and suggested tweaks to chapter 3. Law professors Richard Hasen (University of California–Irvine) and Richard Pildes (New York University) both offered valuable comments on chapter 6. Sam Bagenstos, the law professor at the University of Michigan who argued for the plaintiff in *Young v. UPS,* offered insights and an encouraging review of chapter 7. Alan Morrison, a professor of law at George Washington University, made helpful suggestions for chapter 8. My college professor Stephen Macedo, now at Princeton, offered helpful comments on the introduction and chapter 10. Gary Buseck, legal director of Gay and Lesbian Defenders and Advocates (GLAD), gave me invaluable pointers on chapter 10, and an exchange with Mary Bonauto, the lawyer who argued for marriage equality in *Obergefell v. Hodges,* spurred me to refine that chapter as well.

A very warm acknowledgement to my colleagues at *The Economist,* a publication I'm humbled and delighted to write for. Will Wilkinson drew me in to the world of blogging in 2011, and Roger McShane hit "publish" on my first post at *The Economist* in 2012. Jon Fasman encouraged me to get started covering the court for the print edition; Robert Guest gave me that thrilling opportunity and supported me at every turn. John Prideaux and Emily Bobrow, my current editors, have saved many twisted constructions and misguided arguments from seeing the light of day. They're also delightful bosses. I'd also like to thank Dan Honan, Andrea Chalupa, Marc Perton, Jason Gots, and Peter Hopkins, my editors at Big Think, where I have been blogging blissfully on the courts, American politics, and political theory for the past three-and-a-half years.

Preface

A sabbatical from my position teaching political science at Bard High School Early College in Manhattan enabled me to write this book and to complete several other projects. Many thanks to Principal Michael Lerner, Assistant Principal Camille Sawick, Dean of Studies Siska Brutsaert, and Associate Dean of Studies Bill Hinrichs for supporting the sabbatical from the start. And thank you to my colleagues in the Social Sciences Department (Paula Burleigh, Daniel Freund, Rene Marion, Thomas Martin, Bruce Matthews, Petra Riviere, Veronica Vallejo, and Meghann Walk) for collegiality and encouragement. During the fall 2014 semester, my "Reason and Politics" students spurred me to think through tricky questions in cases covered in chapters 1 and 7, and I am particularly indebted to one of those talented students, Liana Van Nostrand, who read my introduction and many chapter drafts with an eagle eye. She caught errors and asked excellent questions that helped me improve the manuscript.

Finally and most profoundly, I send gratitude and love to my parents, Ingrid and Marvin; parents-in-law, Carol and Joel; siblings, Barb and Jeff; sister-in-law, Carol; brother-in-law, Art; brother-in-law, Aharon, and his gal Nadia; and my wife, Renanit Levy, and our daughters, Amarya (age eleven), Barra (age seven), and Yona (age one), for lively dinnertime conversations about justice and the law—and for absolutely everything else.

The Supreme Court on Trial

In the words of Laurence Tribe, the Harvard law professor who has argued thirty-six cases before the justices, the Supreme Court under Chief Justice John Roberts has been a purveyor of "uncertain justice." Erwin Chemerinsky, a respected Supreme Court litigator and dean of the University of California–Irvine School of Law, develops a "case against the Supreme Court" in his recent book, portraying the institution as "an emperor that truly has no clothes." And in a broader critique, Georgia State law professor Eric Segall maintains that "the Supreme Court does not act like a court and its justices do not decide cases like judges." The institution is closer to "an ultimate political veto council," Segall charges, and its decisions have much more to do with its members' personal or political values than with the law.

These books document ample cause for cynicism. A catalogue of jurisprudential embarrassment is woven into the history of the Supreme Court: *Dred Scott v. Sandford,* a pre–Civil War case drawing blacks out of the circle of American citizenship; *Buck v. Bell,* a 1927 decision authored by Oliver Wendell Holmes upholding the forced sterilization of a low-IQ young woman because "three generations of imbeciles are enough"; and *Korematsu v. United States,* a ruling from 1944 justifying the internment of Japanese Americans in concentration camps along the West Coast of the United States during World War II, to name just three examples. Over the

1

centuries, the justices have propagated what Americans across the ideological spectrum would regard today as an ample share of injustice. And in the past few decades, the court has issued a number of decisions regarding privacy, gun rights, racial equality, sexual liberty, and religion in public life, among others, that have led Americans to view the justices in increasingly ideological, and partisan, terms. The Supreme Court has often drawn criticism in its 226 years, but the darkening cloud over the justices, and the spate of recent negative commentary, can be traced back a decade and a half to the explosive 5–4 *Bush v. Gore* decision that effectively made George W. Bush the nation's forty-third president.

There is much to decry in both the court's deep history and its decisions of recent years. Yet the intense wave of scholarly criticism seems to me—as a political scientist who has studied the court and, more recently, as a journalist who covers its day-to-day machinations—a bit overblown. For all its faults, the Supreme Court has come very far in honing its interpretations of constitutional rights. Even with their profound and often testy internal disagreements—jurisprudential conflicts very much on display in the most-watched cases of October Term 2014—the justices today would universally condemn the decisions in *Dred Scott, Buck,* and *Korematsu.* The conceptions of racial equality and individual liberty that operate in current Supreme Court jurisprudence would foreclose the troubling results reached in each of those cases, as well as many other problematic decisions, such as *Schenck v. United States* and *Dennis v. United States,* cases following World War I and World War II, respectively, in which the justices allowed phantom concerns about national security to take a bite out of the freedom of speech.

This is not to say that the justices get everything, or even most things, right. You do not hold in your hands a hagiography of the court or of any of its members. A couple of years of reading briefs and opinions and sitting in on oral arguments has not turned me into an adoring fan. The justices can be aggressive, petty, snarky, and even (though rarely) ill prepared for hearings. They can badger lawyers, talk over each other, and spin poorly thought-through hypotheticals—or remain inexplicably silent. Their decisions can be too breezily argued, melodramatic, devoid of manners, or needlessly long.

So to what do I owe my moderately upbeat perspective on the court—and on October Term 2014? It stems not from any particular decision or from the particular justices who happen to occupy its nine high-backed, leather-appointed chairs at this historical moment. My optimism stems from how the Supreme Court operates as an institution. The modus operandi of the court dictates much about how the justices go about their work—and more often than not, they do so judiciously, rigorously, and with impressive thoroughness. The process by which the court operates is laid out in an appendix to Garrett Epps's *American Justice 2014* that is well worth perusing. Here is a few-sentence paraphrase: Each year, the justices and their clerks grapple with seven thousand to eight thousand petitions for "certiorari"—requests from parties who lost in a state or federal court below. If at least four justices vote to hear the case (a "grant"), which they have done about seventy to seventy-five times per term in recent years, the lawyers and interested members of the public prepare written briefs—documents that often push seventy or eighty pages explaining why one side or another ought to prevail. The justices read and consider these briefs while readying themselves for what is typically one hour of oral argument—hearings that are open to the press and several hundred members of the public. During the oral hearings, justices pepper lawyers with questions to expose weak points in their arguments and, indirectly, to make their views known to each other. Following oral argument, there is radio silence from the justices while they meet in private conference, vote, and write the opinions. Then decision day arrives, and the justice who wrote the majority opinion reads, with little fanfare, a short statement announcing and briefly explaining the decision. In exceptional cases, dissenters may offer an oral explanation of why they disagree with the majority.

As October Term 2014 swung through the fall's arguments regarding religious and pregnant workers' rights, the separation of powers, race and redistricting, police traffic stops and free speech—and built up to dramatic springtime hearings concerning the death penalty, the fate of Obamacare, and same-sex marriage—I was reminded of a concept central to the work of John Rawls, the great twentieth-century political philosopher who theorized on liberal political societies. Rawls wrote that "public reason" lies at the heart of a liberal democratic order, and the highest court in such a society (he didn't mean the US Supreme Court specifically, though he had it in mind) serves as "the exemplar of public reason."

Given the vast and deep diversity of viewpoints that a large populace encompasses, Rawls writes, it is no mean task to find a way for everyone to speak constructively to one another. Democracy is government by discussion, though, so if people give up on talking to one another because they are always talking *past* one another, the whole enterprise falls apart.

This is why, for Rawls, it is essential that people "consider what kinds of reasons they may reasonably give one another when fundamental political questions are at stake." It is a nonstarter to simply restate your personal religious or moral commitments, as others may not share them. Citizens need to give each other warrants for their claims that their friends, foes, and neighbors could accept without having to fundamentally change who they are or where their metaphysical commitments may lie.

Rawls knows that this all sounds a bit too rosy: it isn't possible for anyone—even a Supreme Court justice—to completely divorce herself from her religious or ideological commitments for the sake of political (or even legal) deliberation. Yet the notion of public reason is an "ideal," in Rawls's terms, and social and political institutions can help model it for the rest of us. As the exemplar of public reason, a supreme court is obligated to ground its rulings in the law and the history of constitutional interpretation and to make a good-faith effort to explain and justify its decisions to the world.

Appreciating the practical force of Rawls's argument admittedly requires some suspension of disbelief. To look at *Bush v. Gore*, or *Burwell v. Hobby Lobby* (the 2014 decision exempting some religiously inspired businesses from the requirement of providing their employees with free birth control), one may reflexively scoff at Rawls's suggestion that "public reason is the sole reason the court exercises." Indeed, Eric Segall makes exactly the opposite claim. The justices serve for life and are transparently motivated by their own values, he argues. They face no constraints from other political actors. Five-to-four decisions like *Bush v. Gore* and *Burwell v. Hobby Lobby* do not have the glow of calm, impartial applications of the law; they appear to reflect the justices' partisan or ideological predilections. The same goes for *Obergefell v. Hodges,* this year's 5–4 same-sex marriage decision, among others.

But don't harrumph and join the cynics too quickly. Keep in mind that Rawls is speaking in idealist terms. In a democracy, the judiciary is indeed "the only branch of government that is visibly on its face the creature of [public] reason and of that reason alone." This is in stark contrast to the "political branches" where legislators are free to vote based on their ideological commitments. "The role of the justices," for Rawls, "is to . . . justify by public reason why they vote as they do." They must decide a case by asking not what they happen to value or what their constituents might want but "what they think the constitutional cases, practices, and traditions, and . . . texts require." The entire procedure leading up to opinion day is suffused with reason-giving and the development and parsing of arguments.

So even if, for example, Justice Alito's real motivation for siding with Hobby Lobby in 2014 was his personal opposition to methods of birth control that some consider abortifacients, he could not write an opinion premised on the contention that IUDs or the morning-after pill are instruments of murder. He has to provide a legal justification. The same goes for Justice Kennedy's vote in OT 2014's *Obergefell v. Hodges:* a constitutional right to same-sex marriage must be grounded in more than a reflexive affinity for gay people. The "task of the justices," Rawls explains, is "to try to develop and express in their reasoned opinions the best interpretation of the constitution they can, using their knowledge of what the constitution and constitutional precedents require." When articulating the grounds for their decisions, the justices' "own personal morality" as well as "other people's religious or philosophical views" are irrelevant. What matters is the law and traditions of its interpretation. To be sure, the justices differ widely in their interpretive methods. They routinely debate how narrowly or expansively a provision of the Constitution should be read, whether one principle or another ought to take precedence in the case of a conflict, or how legislative intent should inform their understanding of a statute. But every justice has a jurisprudence, a theory by which cases should be adjudicated. No matter *what* they decide, by weighing both sides' written and oral arguments and rooting their decisions credibly in public sources, the Supreme Court functions as an exemplar of civility and reasonableness for the rest of us (even if some justices, notably Justice Scalia, too often frame criticisms of their brethren in excessively bitter, and even rude, terms).

One might still argue that this is, at best, wishful thinking. The legal justifications justices come up with may be little more than skillfully drawn fig leaves for their personal values. Segall outlines a number of decisions in his 2012 book where this seems to be the case. But a brief survey of the decisions in October Term 2014 does not bear out such a cynical reading. Rawls knows that justices often will not "agree with one another." And even in an idealized Supreme Court, justices will sometimes reach the wrong result. Most of the cases heard by the Supreme Court are necessarily hard ones on which lower courts have divided and which concern ambiguous statutes or constitutional provisions. Reasonable judges can, and will, disagree. But the justices must nevertheless justify their decisions in terms that the parties to a case and the wider public could, theoretically, understand and accept even if they disagree with the result.

At a talk at the New York Public Library in April 2015, Justice Sonia Sotomayor told the audience that the justices should not be blamed for the purported "politicization" of the court. "The world around us has politicized what we've done," she said. Justice Stephen Breyer fretted in 2010 that "more and more people think that what's important to us is political" and that the court is populated by "nine junior varsity politicians." But, Justice Breyer insists, "that isn't what goes on." Most vocal about perceptions of the court's integrity is John Roberts, the chief justice for the past decade. At his Senate confirmation hearings in 2005, Roberts famously analogized a judge's role to that of a baseball umpire who earnestly calls "balls and strikes" without favoring either side. Like an umpire, he implied, a judge ought to have no skin in the game. In the fall of 2014, the chief justice worried aloud that the increasingly partisan rancor in the judicial confirmation process has pushed the public to construe the court's decisions in increasingly political terms. "I'm worried about people having that perception, because it's not an accurate one," Roberts told an audience at the University of Nebraska. "It's not how we do our work, and it's important that we make that as clear as we can to the public. We're not Republicans or Democrats."

There are a few reasons the court appears to be so partisan. Most obviously, the justices are often asked to confront, and resolve, hugely divisive issues in American politics. Sometimes they demur, but often they agree to take on those questions in order to resolve a circuit split or give Americans an answer to a basic question the other branches of government are not suited to supply. No matter whether they rule for or against affirmative action or a right to gay marriage, for example, the decision will take on a political flavor. Chief Justice Roberts is right to point to the Senate's fevered confirmation process for justices as another culprit. The media are also partly to blame. It's a little reductive and misleading to characterize justices as "liberals" or "conservatives," as those labels can take on so many different meanings in different contexts. But by and large, this is a valid, broadbrush way to distinguish two blocs of justices that divide in fairly reliable ways on controversial questions involving religious rights, racial equality, abortion, gay rights, and the death penalty.

I use the "liberal" and "conservative" language in my own reporting and in this book. But I stay away from describing the justices, as some writers do, as "Republicans" and "Democrats." The justices' party affiliations are irrelevant to their jobs. They do not represent any particular partisan platform when asking questions of lawyers, deciding how to resolve a tough case, or writing an opinion. And it is too cynical by half to say that advancing the cause of either the Democratic Party or the Republican Party is a secret motivation of any of the justices. No one on today's court could be aptly described as a shill for either of the major American political parties.

It is harder to refute charges that the justices are driven by ideological, if not strictly partisan, commitments. But this take is problematic, too. The individuals who serve on the Supreme Court may be swayed, in rendering judgment on the law, by personal commitments or even, as legal philosopher and federal circuit judge Jerome Frank once said, by what they "had for breakfast." But voting patterns in a given term's cases defy easy ideological categorization. Every year, the justices issue more unanimous opinions than 5–4 decisions. October Term 2014 was one of the most divisive in recent years, but the justices still ended up 9–0 in 41 percent of argued cases, as compared to 5–4 splits coming in 29 percent of cases. In October Term 2013, they handed down 9–0 decisions in a whopping 66 percent of argued cases and 5–4 decisions only 14 percent of the time. Dahlia Lithwick of *Slate* memorably christened this phenomenon "fauxnanimity": many 9–0 decisions mask conflicting justifications and perspectives, with fraught concurring opinions that sound more like dissents. But the number of unanimous rulings is still remarkable for a court that is often described as hopelessly divided into rival bloodthirsty jurisprudential gangs.

To read many reports from left-wing or right-wing commentators, the justices are either saints or devils, with few gray areas to be found. They may use legal language to transmit their views, the fervid reporters imply, but the justices are really just imposing their view of what's good or what's right on 320 million Americans. But to watch the proceedings, it just doesn't seem that way. There is no doubt that the court is involved in careful, thorough, serious discourse throughout the certiorari, briefing, argument, and opinion phases of a case. This is the work of "public reason": the justices search the constitutional or statutory text, interpret and apply relevant precedents, and employ logical, reasoned judgment to arrive at a decision.

But how often do we encounter hard evidence that Supreme Court justices aren't mere politicians in robes? It is a common assumption that the court's four "liberals" (Stephen Breyer, Ruth Bader Ginsburg, Elena Kagan, and Sonia Sotomayor) will come down on one side of a case, and the five "conservatives" (Samuel Alito, Anthony Kennedy, John Roberts, Antonin Scalia, and Clarence Thomas) will come down on the other, except when it comes to gay rights cases, where Justice Kennedy reliably joins the liberal side. This characterization tracks Justice Ginsburg's comment to NPR's Nina Totenberg in July 2015 that in recent terms, the court's liberals have tried to speak with one voice on important questions. But none of the justices vote in lockstep. Members of both the liberal and conservative blocs wander from their jurisprudential silos more often than casual observers may realize, and this past term, the conservatives—showing more open-mindedness, perhaps, than the court's left wing—were particularly willing to strike out on their own.

The best evidence of the justices' fair-mindedness comes in surprising questions during oral arguments—when a justice poses a query that seems to run flat against his or her supposed commitments or prejudices—and when a decision is unanimous or features an unusual split of justices. October Term 2014 featured good examples of each:

- In the oral argument in *Texas Department of Housing and Community Affairs v. Inclusive Communities*

Project on January 15, 2015, Justice Scalia, the court's leading critic of the "disparate impact" theory of racial equality, asked a question that seemed to directly contravene his position. The lawyer for Texas was arguing that the Fair Housing Act (FHA) allows lawsuits against only intentional racial discrimination by landlords or developers, not those that are based on possible racial imbalances caused by their actions. But Justice Scalia pointed to the legislative history of the FHA and found evidence that Congress did mean to permit disparate-impact suits. Why, he asked the lawyer, "doesn't that kill your case"? Ultimately, Justice Scalia voted with the conservatives. He never clarified why Texas's case wasn't, in fact, undercut by the FHA's legislative history. But he was open-minded enough to ask the question.

- On December 15, 2014, the 5–4 decision in *Dart Cherokee Basin Operating Company v. Owens,* a case asking what's required for a defendant to move a case from state to federal court, produced a highly unusual split. Justice Ginsburg wrote for two liberals (Breyer and Sotomayor) and two conservatives (Roberts and Alito). In dissent was an odd pairing of three conservatives (Scalia, Thomas, and Kennedy) with arguably the most liberal justice (Kagan).

- The same curious 5–4 split occurred on February 25, 2015, in the colorful case of *Yates v. United States,* a dispute over whether a fisherman's haul of red grouper counts as "tangible objects" that may not be disposed of during a criminal investigation.

Justice Ginsburg wrote the majority opinion; Justice Kagan wrote the dissent.

- On March 9, 2015, the justices unanimously struck down a decision by the District of Columbia Circuit Court in *Perez v. Mortgage Bankers Association.* With strong concurrences from Justices Scalia and Thomas, the nine held that there is no legal duty for federal regulators to invite public comment before they change a regulatory rule.
- In another 9–0 decision that same day, *Department of Transportation v. Association of American Railroads,* the justices put aside differences over the constitutionality of a 2008 law giving Amtrak wide discretion over rules governing use of railroad tracks and concluded that the passenger-train company is part of the government, not a private entity. Justice Thomas wrote a long concurrence criticizing a string of Supreme Court decisions regarding the division of the powers of government.
- On March 25, 2015, in the case of *Young v. UPS* (which I cover in chapter 7), Chief Justice Roberts and Justice Alito broke with their conservative colleagues to join the liberal justices in a ruling that expands antidiscrimination protections for pregnant women in the workplace.
- On April 29, Chief Justice Roberts sided with the court's four liberals against his conservative colleagues for the first time since upholding Obamacare against a constitutional challenge in 2012. The case was *Williams-Yulee v. Florida Bar,*

a dispute over whether the First Amendment permits a rule banning judicial candidates from personally soliciting funds for their campaigns. (I cover it in chapter 2.)

- Justice Alito wrote a concurrence joined by Anthony Kennedy and Sonia Sotomayor—a trio that seldom dances together—in *Reed v. Town of Gilbert*, a 9–0 decision regarding the constitutionality of content-based sign regulations that was announced on June 18, 2015.

- In *Walker v. Sons of Confederate Veterans*, a 5–4 ruling also released on June 18 (and which I cover in chapter 2), ultraconservative Justice Thomas joined the four liberal justices against his conservative brethren to allow Texas to refuse to issue a specialty license plate featuring the Confederate flag.

- Justice Kennedy broke from his conservative colleagues not only in the same-sex marriage case (which he authored) but in four other significant cases: *King v. Burwell* (the challenge to Obamacare), *Texas Department of Housing and Community Affairs v. Inclusive Communities Project* (the disparate-impact case), *Alabama Legislative Black Caucus v. Alabama* (a race and redistricting case covered in chapter 6), and *Arizona State Legislature v. Arizona Independent Redistricting Commission* (a gerrymandering case also analyzed in chapter 6). Chief Justice Roberts, too, joined the court's liberals in saving Obamacare from implosion.

I cite these examples not to propose that any of the justices are free of bias. They all have jurisprudential proclivities that push them in rather reliably predictable directions in many cases. But along the way to the resolution of a case, the justices do not seem to put ideology before a commitment to the law. They are generally (with more than a few exceptions, which I note in the chapters to come) fair-minded and thorough, or at least they appear to be. They render judgments in argued cases with carefully wrought opinions. And they break the stereotypical mold more often than the court-watcher who reads only the front-page stories could notice.

The ten chapters of *American Justice 2015* are organized thematically, beginning with cases involving religious freedom and ending with the term's marriage equality decision. In the first four chapters, I proceed more or less in order of the constitutional rights protected in the Constitution's amendments even if they involve, as a technical matter, statutory questions.

Chapter 1 considers two cases in which Muslim Americans—one a prisoner, the other a job applicant— prevailed in their claims of religious discrimination. Chapter 2 looks at three interestingly different cases implicating the First Amendment right to the freedom of speech. In chapter 3, I turn to two cases inquiring into the constitutionality, under the Fourth Amendment, of unorthodox traffic stops by police. Chapter 4 moves on to the Eighth Amendment to analyze a case asking whether a particular combination of execution drugs violates the ban on "cruel and unusual punishments." Chapter 5 looks at the constitutional value of equality as enshrined in the Fourteenth Amendment through an analysis of the Fair Housing Act and whether the adverse impacts on minorities, rather than just biased motivations of developers or lenders, can be used to prove racial discrimination.

Chapter 6 looks at two cases involving voting and democracy: one concerning racial gerrymandering in Alabama, the other an attempt in Arizona to take redistricting out of the hands of state legislators. In chapter 7, I consider a gender equality case asking how a law that bans pregnancy discrimination applies to the plight of a pregnant UPS driver who requested and was denied temporary light duty. Chapter 8 looks at this term's major separation-of-powers case, in which the justices expanded presidential power to conduct certain types of foreign policy. And in chapters 9 and 10, I treat the two blockbuster cases concerning Obamacare and the right of same-sex marriage: historic decisions with profound social, economic, and political implications.

Finally, the epilogue sketches the issues awaiting us in October Term 2015. Looming cases involving abortion, affirmative action, public unions, criminal justice, and the right to vote foretell another year in which the Supreme Court will play an outsize role in shaping the nation's future.

Freedom of Religion: The Religious Liberty of Inmates and Employees

Holt v. Hobbs; Equal Employment Opportunity Commission v. Abercrombie & Fitch Stores

It was the year of the Muslim at the Supreme Court. During October Term 2013, conservative Christians won Supreme Court battles over the constitutionality of monthly town-board prayers (*Town of Greece v. Galloway*) and the enforceability of the Affordable Care Act's contraceptive mandate on certain religious employers (*Burwell v. Hobby Lobby*). But in October Term 2014, American Catholics and evangelical Protestants had no religious-liberty cases before the justices. (They did win *Reed v. Town of Gilbert*, a case involving municipal sign regulations, but that concerned the freedom of speech.) Instead, in OT 2014, the religious beliefs of two American Muslims took center stage.

The individuals in question could not be more different. Samantha Elauf was a seventeen-year-old Oklahoma woman whose traditional headscarf, or hijab, cost her a job at a kids' branch of clothing retailer Abercrombie & Fitch in 2008. Gregory Holt, who adopted the name Abdul

Maalik Muhammad after his conversion to Islam in 2011, was serving time in an Arkansas prison for stabbing his girlfriend in the course of an altercation between the two. He claimed that the prison's grooming policy prevented him from fulfilling a religious duty to grow a beard. Neither Elauf nor Holt relied on the First Amendment's free exercise clause to stake their claims. Elauf's case was one of employment discrimination, focused on the meaning of Title VII of the Civil Rights Act of 1964, while Holt brought his complaint under the Religious Land Use and Institutionalized Persons Act (RLUIPA), a law Congress passed unanimously in 2000 to protect prisoners and churches from behavioral rules and zoning regulations that impinged on their religious interests.

Holt v. Hobbs

On October 7, the second day of oral arguments in October Term 2014, the Supreme Court heard its first religious liberty case since recognizing the right of pious employers to deny birth control coverage to their employees in *Burwell v. Hobby Lobby* the previous June. At issue was whether the grooming policy at the Arkansas Department of Corrections, which regards beards as "opportunities for disguise and for transport of contraband and weapons," violated RLUIPA, which says that prisons may only prohibit inmates' religious conduct if there is a "compelling governmental interest" at stake and they use the "least restrictive means" of doing so.

In light of the quarter-inch beards Arkansas permits for inmates with dermatological problems and noting that forty-four other state and federal prison systems allow their inmates to grow beards, Holt's lawyer, Douglas Laycock, an expert in religious liberty and a professor at the University of Virginia law school, contended the state had no good reason to fight the stubble. While prison officials are due a degree of deference, he argued, they need to provide "a reasoned and well-considered and informed explanation" for policies that interfere with inmates' rights. After a relatively smooth turn for Laycock, David Curran, the deputy attorney general of Arkansas, took the lectern. It was clear early in his thirty minutes that Curran would have a tough time defending the prison's policy.

Justice Alito, the court's staunchest defender of the freedom of religious exercise, proved to be Curran's toughest questioner. In 1999, seven years before he was promoted to the Supreme Court by President George W. Bush, Alito issued a decision as a judge on the Third Circuit Court of Appeals that spoke directly to the issue in *Holt*. Then-judge Alito ruled that the Newark police department could not prevent two Muslim officers from growing beards for religious reasons. Given that the officers with medical justifications were permitted to grow beards, Alito wrote, "[w]e are at a loss to understand why religious exemptions threaten important city interests but medical exemptions do not." The department policy, he ruled, "cannot be sustained."

Given this, Curran should have been better prepared for Justice Alito's sharp questioning. He took aim first at Curran's contention that shifting facial hair patterns make prisoners dangerously unrecognizable to prison officials. When Curran warned that with an option to grow a beard, "an inmate could get into the barracks where he is not supposed to be" after working out in the fields, Justice Alito traced the highly unlikely sequence of events that would facilitate such a ruse: "While he's out there, he shaves, then he wants to come back and go into barracks B. And how's he going to get into barracks B if he has an ID that says barracks A? Now you say he's going to trade with another prisoner? Then he will have a different picture on the ID . . . they're going to alter the IDs also while they're out there in the fields?" In response, Curran could only say, "Prisoners are capable of doing a lot of mischief in prison."

Next, Justice Alito dove into the contraband rationale for the policy. Here Curran seemed almost embarrassed by his own brief's contention that half-inch beards provided prisoners with handy places to stash darts, razors, and SIM cards. "[W]hy can't the prison just give the inmate a comb?" Justice Alito proposed, drawing laughter in the courtroom. "If there's a SIM card in there or . . . a tiny revolver . . . it'll fall out."

After the oral argument, the question was not *whether* Holt would prevail but if there were *any* justices willing to vote against him. The answer came on January 20, 2015. In a unanimous decision, the court ruled that although RLUIPA "affords prison officials ample ability to maintain security," it requires officials to demonstrate that a rule substantially burdening an inmate's religion is actually necessary. "The Department has failed to show," Justice Alito's opinion read, "that its policy is the least restrictive means of furthering its compelling interests."

The analysis in the *Holt* decision was clear and straightforward; Justice Alito's opinion ran a modest sixteen pages. The direct implications were not very far-reaching: the case liberates inmates in six states to grow religiously inspired half-inch beards. So a few pious incarcerated whiskers may see the light of day as a result. The case has broader significance, however.

Justice Alito's opinion clarifies the rather extraordinary expansion of religious liberty that has occurred under RLUIPA—both for inmates and for their odd-bedfellow statutory cousins, religious institutions. And it reinforces the breadth of the "compelling interest test" that RLUIPA shares with the Religious Freedom Restoration Act (RFRA), the 1993 statute under which religious corporations, in the *Hobby Lobby* ruling, won an exemption from Obamacare's contraceptive mandate.

This pair of religious rights laws was passed in the wake *Employment Division v. Smith,* a deeply unpopular Supreme Court ruling from 1990 in which Justice Scalia significantly dialed back the protections available to individuals under the Constitution's free exercise clause. In *Smith,* Alfred Smith and Galen Black had lost their jobs at a drug rehabilitation facility for taking peyote, a hallucinogenic drug, during their (off-the-job) Native American Church rites. When Smith and Black applied for unemployment compensation, Oregon turned them down on the grounds that they had been fired for misconduct. The men then sued, winning in the Oregon Supreme Court but ultimately losing in the US Supreme Court. Justice Scalia's majority opinion stated that neutral laws of general applicability—like Oregon's drug statutes—are not unconstitutional since they do not treat religious beliefs or rituals differently from similar acts done for secular reasons. While states *may* offer religious exemptions to generally applicable laws, Justice Scalia wrote, they *need not* do so.

The reaction from Congress was swift and decisive. RFRA, passed unanimously in the House and by a vote of 97–3 in the Senate, restored the broader protections that reigned in the nearly three decades bookended by *Sherbert v. Verner,* the 1963 case laying out the "compelling interest" test, and *Smith.* But RFRA soon faced challenges of its own, and in 1997, the Supreme Court ruled, in *City of Boerne v. Flores,* that the law was unconstitutional as applied to state and local governments. Section 5 of the Fourteenth Amendment, Justice Anthony Kennedy wrote for the 6–3 majority, did not authorize Congress to enact such restrictions against the states. To partially repair the hole left by *City of Boerne,* Congress then passed RLUIPA to protect prisoners and religious institutions.

Justice Ginsburg signed on to Justice Alito's opinion in *Holt* but wrote separately to distinguish Holt's request to grow a beard from Hobby Lobby's request for an exemption from the contraceptive mandate of the Affordable Care Act in *Burwell v. Hobby Lobby.* In *Hobby Lobby,* on the final day of October Term 2013, the owners of the crafts store were granted the exemption by a 5–4 vote. As evangelical Christians, David Green and his family members asserted that they could not, in good conscience, pay to supply their employees with birth control devices and drugs they considered to be abortifacients. Justice Ginsburg filed a fiery, full-throated dissent in *Hobby Lobby.* Her central contention was that the majority refused to consider "the impact that accommodation may have on third parties who do not share the corporation owners' religious faith." So in *Holt v. Hobbs,* she felt the need to explain why beards in prison are different from contraceptive coverage at work. "Unlike the exemption this Court approved in *Burwell v. Hobby Lobby Stores,*" she wrote, "accommodating petitioner's religious beliefs in this case would not detrimentally affect others who do not share petitioner's beliefs."

Part of the court's investigation in considering whether to grant religious exemptions from generally applicable laws, as in *Hobby Lobby,* or from prison grooming regulations, as in *Holt,* is whether and in what way the accommodation will impact the lives of other people. No one suffers when Holt lets his stubble grow a bit. But when a corporation with twenty-three thousand employees refuses to provide a benefit available under federal law, thousands of women are directly impacted. In the typical case, they would have to buy their own birth control pills or shell out $1,000 for an IUD. The *Hobby Lobby* majority maintained that this was not the typical case, because the government had already devised a reliable means for providing free contraception to all female employees without requiring the employer to pay for it, contract for it, or arrange for it. The impact on employees, according to the majority, would be "precisely zero," though the dissenters did not see it that way.

In a case from 1985, *Estate of Thornton v. Caldor, Inc.,* the Supreme Court struck down a law granting every employee the right not to come in to work on his or her Sabbath. This law, the justices found, constituted a "substantial burden" on employers, who had to offer higher pay to persuade workers to come in on the weekend. And it represented a "significant burden" on nonreligious employees who had to fill in for their Sabbath-observant colleagues: "The unyielding weighting in favor of Sabbath observers over all other interests contravenes a fundamental principle of the Religion Clauses: the First Amendment gives no one the right to insist that in pursuit of their own interests others must conform their conduct to his own religious necessities."

Ian Millhiser overstated things when he wrote at *Think Progress* that Justice Ginsburg's *Holt* concurrence, in line with the reasoning in *Caldor*, is "everything you need to know about religious liberty." While there are cases like *Hobby Lobby* and *Holt* in which an accommodation either does or doesn't bring harm to third parties, there are plenty of cases that are more difficult to classify.

No one appears to be harmed when a Seventh-Day Adventist gets an unemployment check after being fired for refusing to come to work on Saturday. But think again: taxpayers foot that bill. And it's not quite true that nobody is negatively affected when the Amish win an exemption from mandatory schooling laws after the eighth grade, as they did in *Wisconsin v. Yoder* in 1972. What about the children who have their education (and therefore career and life opportunities) cut short? And what about the wider society, which may benefit if talented Amish people opt for a life outside the church? Should the interests of these third parties factor into the analysis when religious people request exemptions?

Not all impacts on third parties, like adding a penny to everybody's tax bill in order accommodate the Seventh-Day Adventist, are specific or onerous enough to be truly worrisome. But it is hard to pinpoint at which stage the burden becomes a problem worth worrying about. Those seeking clarity for future claims of religious free exercise will not find it in Justice Ginsburg's haiku-like concurrence in *Holt*. Nor will they reach a clear answer by studying the majority opinions in *Holt* or *Hobby Lobby*. But moving forward, it seems clear that the accommodations of religious individuals' special requests under RFRA and RLUIPA will be uneasy and may conflict with another provision from the First Amendment: the establishment clause, which prohibits official state support for religion and preferential treatment for religious people. As Brooklyn Law School professor Nelson Tebbe said in his testimony before the House Judiciary Committee on February 13, 2015, "Costs incurred by protecting religious liberty should be paid by the government or the public, not by other private citizens." Professor Tebbe recommends that RFRA and RLUIPA be amended to clarify that they do not sanction accommodations for corporate entities or exemptions that "would result in meaningful harm to identifiable third parties."

EEOC v. Abercrombie & Fitch Stores

Samantha Elauf was seventeen when, in 2008, she applied for a job selling children's clothes at a branch of Abercrombie Kids in Tulsa, Oklahoma. Elauf had begun wearing a "hijab," the traditional Muslim headscarf, a few years earlier, and she wore it to her Abercrombie interview, along with jeans and a t-shirt. The meeting went well, and Elauf earned solid marks from Heather Cooke, the interviewer, for the categories "appearance and sense of style," "outgoing and promotes diversity," and "sophistication and aspiration." Her scores were high enough to secure the job.

But when Cooke mentioned Elauf's black headscarf to a manager, she was instructed to lower the applicant's "appearance" score and deny her the position. The company's "look policy," which requires employees to adopt the "preppy look of the Ivy League," bars them from wearing "caps" or black clothing. A friend of Elauf had mentioned the look policy to her before her interview, but Abercrombie never told her that her headscarf violated the rules.

Elauf turned to the Equal Employment Opportunity Commission (EEOC), which sued the store on her behalf. A federal district court in Oklahoma ruled that in refusing to hire Elauf because of her religious practice, Abercrombie had violated the rule in Title VII of the Civil Rights Act of 1964 barring employers from failing to hire someone because of "race, color, religion, sex or national origin." On appeal, the Tenth Circuit court reversed and held for the company. The onus of offering a religious accommodation was not on Abercrombie, the Tenth Circuit held. If Elauf needed an exemption from the look policy, she should have asked for it—even if she didn't know she needed it, because Abercrombie had not told her that her headscarf violated any policy.

The crux of the disagreement in *Abercrombie* involved whether the employee or the employer had the responsibility to initiate a discussion about religious accommodation. Does the job applicant have to alert the interviewer to religious beliefs or practices that conflict with workplace policies? Or must the employer proactively offer an exemption from those policies upon inferring that an applicant needs one unless, as the law says, doing so would pose "undue hardship" on the business? Abercrombie said that since Elauf did not explain the significance of her hijab or request an exception from the no-hats policy, the store was under no obligation to hire her. The company also contended that giving Elauf a pass on the policy would make it impossible to do business in the breezy, East Coast prep-school style that defined its merchandise. In the oral argument on February 25, 2015, two unlikely allies, Justice Kagan and Justice Alito, teamed up to demonstrate exactly what was wrong with the store's position. Justice Alito posed a reality-check hypothetical, calling into question Abercrombie's faux-naive contention that it didn't know Elauf would require a look-policy accommodation. "All right," he began. "Let's say four people show up for a job interview at Abercrombie. And this is going to sound like a joke, but, you know, it's not. (Laughter.) So the first is a Sikh man wearing a turban, the second is a Hasidic man wearing a hat, the third is a Muslim woman wearing a hijab, the fourth is a Catholic nun in a habit. Now, do you think . . . that those people have to say, '*We just want to tell you, we're dressed this way for a religious reason. We're not just trying to make a fashion statement?*'"

Shay Dvoretzky, the company's lawyer, could muster only a rather weak hedge: "One can certainly imagine cases in which it is more obvious than others that a particular . . . garb is likely worn for religious purposes." And it *wasn't* clear, he insisted to an incredulous Justice Alito, that Elauf's headscarf really was a hijab. (Cooke's testimony at the district court that she "figured that the headscarf signified that it was a religious headscarf," as Deputy Solicitor General Ian Gershengorn said in his defense of the EEOC position, pretty clearly undercut Dvoretzky's claim.) A few minutes later, Justice Alito sliced to the crux of the matter. "The reason that she was rejected," he said to Dvoretzky, "was because you assumed she was going to do this every day and the only reason why she would do it every day is because she had a religious reason."

Justice Kagan was just as cutting in her take-down of another of Dvoretzky's arguments. Asking employers to offer a reasonable accommodation for religious beliefs and practices when they "correctly understand" one to be necessary, Dvoretzky argued, inevitably promotes stereotyping and problematic inquiries into applicants' religious beliefs. Justices Alito and Sotomayor easily exposed that as a canard: simply letting applicants know about the policy and asking if they would have any trouble abiding by it involves no intrusive questioning about religious beliefs.

But even *if* the discussions were a little intrusive, Justice Kagan asked, isn't it worth the cost? "[Y]ou're essentially saying that the problem with the rule is that it requires Abercrombie to engage in what might be thought of as an awkward conversation, to ask some questions," Justice Kagan said. "Now, people can disagree about whether one can ask those questions in a way that's awkward at all, but you're saying we should structure the whole legal system to make sure that there is no possibility of that awkward conversation ever taking place . . . [B]etween . . . the option of using a stereotype to make sure that somebody never gets a job and using a stereotype to have an awkward conversation, which does this statute seem to think is the worst problem?"

After the Alito-Kagan one-two punch, Justice Breyer entered the ring to clarify Abercrombie's position and deliver a knockout: "Okay. I got you. Is this right? . . . There are millions of people who are practicing one religion or another where you get a clue of that from their name or maybe their dress or whatever it is. And whenever we have such a person applying, if she doesn't say anything . . . and we don't hire them or we don't do it, we're going to get sued. And we don't want all those lawsuits . . . Have I got the essence of your message?"

Dvoretzky's reply to the Socratic interrogation—"That's right"—brought a broad smile to Justice Breyer's face. He had led his interlocutor right where he wanted him to go. The bottom line is that the company fought the EEOC for one reason only: because it doesn't want to have to worry about being sued for religious discrimination. The manager knew very well that Elauf was a Muslim woman who needed an accommodation for her hijab under Title VII. But instead of offering that exemption, he simply refused to hire her.

At the hearing, a majority of the justices gave the distinct impression they would uphold Elauf's claim against her would-be employer. And on June 1, 2015, that impression was confirmed. In a lopsided 8–1 decision, with only Justice Clarence Thomas dissenting, the Supreme Court clarified that Title VII requires employers to offer reasonable accommodations to applicants and employees when company policies chafe against their religious scruples.

Justice Scalia wrote an uncharacteristically concise seven-page majority opinion. It was, he said from the bench, a "really easy" decision. Scalia first rejected "Abercrombie's primary argument" that no breach of Title VII is possible unless "an employer has 'actual knowledge' of the applicant's need for an accommodation." Whether or not the applicant has informed him of a religious practice that requires accommodation, Scalia held, an employer breaks the law if this inference "was a motivating factor" in the employer's decision.

A fair question here would be how the needed accommodation could possibly be a "motivating factor" in an employer's decision to reject an applicant if the employer had no knowledge of the need in the first place. Justice Scalia clarified that the employer must at least have a semblance of a clue about the nature of the applicant's religious life. But "whether this motive derives from actual knowledge, a well-founded suspicion, or merely a hunch," an employer who won't be bothered to accommodate the religious practice illegally discriminates against the applicant when he refuses to hire her.

Writing in concurrence but with a snarl, Justice Alito frowned on the knowledge-hunch distinction in the majority opinion. If Title VII really "does not impose a knowledge requirement," he wrote, "it would be irrelevant in this case whether Abercrombie had any inkling that Elauf is a Muslim or that she wore the headscarf for a religious reason. That would be very strange." Without a knowledge requirement, employers would face lawsuits for rejecting applicants on a basis they had no idea was religious. Not all religions are as well known as Islam and Judaism, after all.

Consider the Church of the Flying Spaghetti Monster, for example. (I am not making this up.) The official headwear of this church is a colander: yes, the hole-studded bowl used for draining pasta and washing fruit. If a job candidate at an investment bank shows up to his interview with a colander on his head, the interviewer may well balk, misinterpreting the religious garb as a sign the applicant is, even in a charitable view, loopy. But if the applicant doesn't land the job because he was wearing a kitchen utensil as a hat, the bank, under the majority's view, may have violated the candidate's civil rights. Justice Alito suggests, sensibly, that this is deeply unfair: "[A]n employer cannot be held liable for taking an adverse action because of an employee's religious practice unless the employer knows that the employee engages in the practice for a religious reason."

Justice Thomas's dissent was based on the contention that Abercrombie's look policy was neutral with regard to religion—that is, the retailer was not targeting Muslims when it drew up the dress code, and it was not taking aim at Samantha Elauf when it denied her a position at Abercrombie Kids. The company was evenhandedly applying its policy regarding employee dress, Justice Thomas wrote, letting the chips fall where they may. The policy may have fallen more heavily on Elauf, and it may burden certain religions more than others, but this is not by design. Intentional discrimination requires proof of intent to discriminate.

With her win, Samantha Elauf earned a chance to recover the money she was awarded at trial and then denied in the appeals court. But on July 20, less than two months after the Supreme Court's decision, the EEOC and Abercrombie revealed they had settled their differences out of court. The company agreed to pay Elauf $25,670.53 in damages and $18,983.03 in court costs, and a spokesperson noted that Abercrombie was "pleased to have resolved this matter . . . and to be moving forward." The retailer claims it "remains focused on ensuring the company has an open-minded and tolerant workplace environment for all current and future store associates."

Chapter 1

The decision in *EEOC v. Abercrombie* requires employers to be on the lookout for potential conflicts between their policies and the religious lives of their employees. The best approach in an interview may be to ask a version of the question Justice Alito suggested during the oral argument. After laying out company policies with regard to dress, attendance, and so on, the interviewer could simply ask, "Would you have any problem complying with these rules?" If the applicant has a religious scruple that requires accommodation via an exemption from one of the policies, this would be the perfect opening to lay it on the table and discuss it. And if the candidate for the position says, "Sure, that all sounds fine," the employer successfully immunizes himself against a claim of religious discrimination.

Freedom of Speech: Threats, Judges, and License Plates

*Elonis v. United States; Williams-Yulee v. Florida Bar;
Walker v. Texas Division, Sons of Confederate Veterans*

"It is imperative," John Stuart Mill wrote in 1859, "that human beings should be free to form opinions and to express their opinions without reserve." For Mill, free speech is crucial to truth-seeking: errors inevitably lurk in conventional wisdom, and it often takes a dissenter to expose them. For the American Founding Fathers, freedom of speech was the basis of democracy. Without the right to speak one's mind, government by discussion is impossible. But the bedrock principle of American government that "Congress shall make no law . . . abridging the freedom of speech" is not crystalline. Over the centuries, the Supreme Court's understanding of the First Amendment's command has become increasingly complex and occasionally inscrutable. Even the justices sometimes seem flummoxed by the difference between speech limits based on "viewpoint" (nearly always prohibited) and those based on "content" (more often allowed). They disagree on what counts as "speech" and how to determine if it is being illegitimately abridged.

The basic picture, affirmed over the past decade by a highly speech-protective Roberts court, is fairly clear: the government generally may not silence or punish people for expressing themselves, whether the expression is communicated verbally, in writing, in pictures, or in some other form and whether or not the ideas are political, coherent, or tasteful. Yet this blanket protection has its thinner patches. In *Brandenberg v. Ohio,* a 1969 case in which the court upheld a Ku Klux Klan leader's hateful expression, Justice William O. Douglas wrote that "speech brigaded with action" lacks absolute First Amendment refuge. Certain categories of speech, the court has held, are eligible for reduced protection, or none at all. Obscenity, fighting words (speech that incites someone to punch you in the face), "true threats," malicious lies intended to damage someone's reputation (libel), false advertising, and urging someone to take up arms against the government are all seen by the court as expression that can, in fact, be abridged.

During October Term 2014, a trio of speech cases took the justices deep into the First Amendment thicket. *Elonis v. United States* asked what constitutes a "true threat" in the Internet age. In *Walker v. Texas Division, Sons of Confederate Veterans,* the court delineated a boundary between private speech and government-sponsored speech on automobile license plates. And *Williams-Yulee v. Florida Bar* asked whether a Florida rule prohibiting judicial candidates from personally soliciting campaign funds violates their freedom of speech.

Elonis v. United States

Fights over free speech in the United States don't always produce made-for-TV poster children. A century ago, political dissenters turned to the First Amendment as a shield against prosecution for distributing antiwar pamphlets (*Schenck v. United States,* 1919) or publishing socialist magazines (*Gitlow v. New York,* 1925). In recent decades, marauders for free speech have become rather less refined in their messages: racists, antigay activists, pornographers, anti-Semites, dogfight filmmakers, and cross-burners are the new bearers of the free-speech flame.

The most recent First Amendment crusader, Anthony Elonis, is every bit as charming as the petitioners on that esteemed list. Elonis appealed all the way up to the Supreme Court to challenge his 2011 conviction and prison sentence for a series of Facebook posts that a jury determined were threats against his estranged wife and others. The test for determining whether a threat is a "true" one, most courts have held, is not whether the threat materializes. Nor is it whether the speaker meant to carry out the promised act. The question is whether the stated threat, independent of motive or actual result, has the potential to cause panic. In one post, twenty-seven-year-old Elonis wrote, "If I only knew then what I know now . . . I would have smothered your ass with a pillow. Dumped your body in the back seat. Dropped you off in Toad Creek and made it look like a rape and murder." In another missive, Elonis noted:

> There's one way to love ya, but a thousand ways to kill ya,
> And I'm not going to rest until your body is a mess,

Soaked in blood and dying from all the little cuts.
Hurry up and die bitch.

In the oral argument on December 1, 2014, Justice Antonin Scalia asked Michael Dreeben, the government's lawyer, "[T]his language is not worth a whole lot anyway, right?" Freedom of speech offers a safe harbor against laws or officials seeking to punish dissenters or silence unpopular views. By freeing public discussion and debate, it makes self-government possible. But it is hard to imagine what value the Founding Fathers might find in Elonis's crude, albeit colorful, threats.

The petitioner's ex-wife, Tara, certainly did not celebrate Elonis's poetry. In 2010, she won a protection-from-abuse order against him, prompting Elonis to return to his keyboard to compose ever more threatening Facebook posts. When he expanded his targets to elementary-school students and an FBI agent, Elonis was charged, convicted, and sentenced to forty-four months in prison.

The federal jury was tasked with determining whether Elonis's posts could be understood by a reasonable observer as serious plans to inflict harm. This is the legal test used in most jurisdictions, though in two federal districts and some states, the standard is subjective and therefore harder to prove, asking whether the speaker *actually intended* to cause another person harm. In his brief to the justices and in the hearing, Elonis denied ever having the intention of hurting anybody. His creative outpouring was "therapeutic," he said. It was his way of coping after a traumatic divorce. The posts may have been graphic, but they were only words, and free expression is protected by the First Amendment.

The justices' mission at the December 1, 2014, oral argument was to get a handle on whether the speaker's intent or the listener's interpretation ought to count in defining a threat. But problems with both standards seemed to give the nine a headache.

Justice Alito seemed quite unsympathetic to Elonis's position. The abusive husband's defense that he was just throwing together some rap lyrics and meant no harm is a "roadmap for threatening a spouse and getting away with it." But other justices worried that upholding Elonis's conviction would sharply curtail First Amendment freedoms. "Mr. Dreeben," Justice Kagan said, "we typically say that the First Amendment requires a kind of a buffer zone to ensure that even stuff that is wrongful maybe is permitted because we don't want to chill innocent behavior."

In an exchange with John Elwood, Elonis's lawyer, Justice Kagan explored whether some plausible middle ground might be found: "How about you just take it a step down more but not get to the government's [standard of actual intent to cause harm]. How about if you don't know to a certainty, but you know that there is a substantial probability that you will place that person in fear, which is what I take it we would usually mean when we talk about recklessness?"

The "recklessness" standard requires a notch of proof above mere "negligence." Whereas a negligent speaker might not realize his words will be taken as an actual threat, a reckless speaker knows in advance that his speech might be frightening, even if he doesn't actually intend it as such. Should this be the test for whether a true threat has been communicated?

Chapter 2

The third way proved unpopular on both sides. Elwood said it would offer no protection for teenagers "shooting off their mouths or making . . . ill-timed, sarcastic comments which wind up getting them thrown in jail," since they *could* have realized in advance that their words had the potential to frighten. Dreeben's worry was that a recklessness test "basically immunizes somebody who makes [a threat] and then can plausibly say later, 'hey, I was dead drunk, I realized that I just called in a bomb threat and the police had to respond and an elementary school had to be evacuated and I knew what I was saying but I was too drunk'" to sense that authorities may interpret the joke as an actual threat.

Chief Justice John Roberts wondered what distinguishes Elonis's diatribes from the brutally violent lyrics rapper Eminem sings on his multiplatinum records. The difference, according to Dreeben, is that Eminem's aggressive musings are delivered "at a concert where people are going to be entertained." But it seems absurd to say that entertainment value is the litmus test for determining what counts as constitutionally protected speech.

As the head of what is probably the most speech-protective court in Supreme Court history, Chief Justice Roberts was left in something of a pickle. On the one hand, he had a truly despicable defendant who terrorized his wife and other innocent bystanders with his online posts. A ruling favorable to Elonis may make it more difficult to prosecute domestic violence charges. But on the other hand, upholding Elonis's conviction may give the government license to punish people for experimenting a little too freely on their Facebook pages. That seems decidedly out of line with the spirit of the First Amendment.

The Supreme Court's decision, announced on June 1, 2015, a full six months after the oral hearing, showed signs of the chief's furrowed brow at work. Roberts clearly wished to avoid the Scylla of giving Elonis a First Amendment pass for his threats, but he was evidently even more eager to steer clear of the Charybdis of imposing new limits on the freedom of speech.

In a majority opinion signed by seven justices, Roberts cleverly found a way to avoid touching the First Amendment at all. He wrote a decision focused squarely on the federal threats law prohibiting "any communication containing any threat . . . to injure the person of another." The Third Circuit Court of Appeals, Roberts wrote, had used the wrong standard in the jury instructions. A criminal conviction requires some level of subjective intent on the part of the speaker. Merely asking how a reasonable person would hear an expression is not sufficient. "Elonis's conviction," Roberts wrote, "was premised solely on how his posts would be understood by a reasonable person. Such a . . . standard is a familiar feature of civil liability in tort law, but is inconsistent with 'the conventional requirement for criminal conduct—awareness of some wrongdoing.'" In sum, "wrongdoing must be conscious to be criminal."

To the consternation of both Justice Alito, who concurred in part and dissented in part, and Justice Thomas, who dissented, the majority opinion remained agnostic on what level of intent is enough to prosecute someone under the threats law. Justice Alito was ready to apply the recklessness standard that came up during the oral argument. When he accused the majority of sowing "confusion" in the lower courts by not stating a view,

Chief Justice Roberts coolly demurred. The standard had not been briefed by either party, he wrote, and no split in the lower courts compelled the Supreme Court to weigh in. It would violate the court's typical "prudence" to decide "what sort of mental element is requisite to a constitutionally permissible prosecution" before such a question is thoroughly investigated in lower-court litigation.

It was a characteristically brilliant escape for the chief, a bit reminiscent of a landmark ruling Chief Justice John Marshall crafted 212 years earlier. In a similarly wily opinion in *Marbury v. Madison,* Marshall managed to get out of a very tough spot. Facing a conundrum in which the court risked losing face (by giving in to Thomas Jefferson, the new president and Marshall's rival) or losing all power (if Jefferson refused to act on the court's decision), Marshall greatly amplified his court's power by handing a nominal win to President Jefferson but claiming a much bigger prize his nemesis was in no position to resist: the power of judicial review. *Elonis v. U.S.* won't have nearly the far-reaching consequences of *Marbury,* to put it very mildly, but it is based in the same style of jurisprudential cunning. Without chipping away at the First Amendment or giving an abusive ex-husband a free pass, the decision permits a lower court to revisit Elonis's misbehavior under new instructions.

Walker v. Texas Division, Sons of Confederate Veterans

"I disapprove of what you say, but I will defend to the death your right to say it": it's a line often attributed to Voltaire, the French philosopher, but in reality, it was penned in 1906 by Voltaire's biographer, Beatrice Evelyn Hall. Hall's summary of Voltaire's position captures the heart of America's free-speech jurisprudence. The principle explains why the Supreme Court permitted the National Socialist Party of America to march down a street in Skokie, Illinois, home to many Holocaust survivors, in 1977 (though the neo-Nazi group later decided to change the venue). It captures why the court frowned on a law prohibiting the burning of the American flag in 1989. And it accounts nicely for Justice Breyer's strategy of pragmatic avoidance in *Walker v. Texas Division, Sons of Confederate Veterans,* a case involving a lightning-rod symbol of America's legacy of slavery, the Confederate flag.

The controversy in *Walker* began in 2009, when the Sons of Confederate Veterans, an association of male descendants of soldiers who fought in the Confederate army during the Civil War, asked the state of Texas to issue a specialty license plate featuring its logo: a square Confederate battle flag framed by the words "Sons of Confederate Veterans 1896" with an octagon surrounding the image and words. In its amicus brief to the court, the American Civil Liberties Union (ACLU) acknowledged the public outcry that resulted when the Sons made the proposal: more than thirty thousand complaints against the "racist relic" flew into the DMV's mailbox, and many state officials joined in the condemnation. The state's governor, 2016 GOP presidential contender Rick Perry, weighed in, saying, "[W]e don't need to be scraping old wounds." In light of this chorus of criticism, the board charged with reviewing applications voted unanimously to reject the Sons' plate. This, the ACLU argued, was a mistake. A license plate with a Confederate flag "undoubtedly evokes strong emotions in the public," but the "eminently under-standable" reason for keeping the Confederate flag off of Texas license plates was nevertheless "an unconstitutional basis for rejecting [the Sons'] message."

The oral argument seemed to leave the justices in a bind. Allowing Texas to reject the proposal would seem to invite all manner of worrisome censorship. But requiring it to print the Confederate flag on license plates may bring any number of offensive and racist symbols to Texas roadways.

The hardest question for the Texas solicitor general, Scott Keller, came from Justice Kagan: "Suppose some-body submitted a license plate to Texas that said, 'Vote Republican,' and Texas said, yes, that's fine. And then the next person submitted a license plate to Texas and it said, 'Vote Democratic,' and Texas said, no, we're not going to approve that one. What about that?" Keller was caught off guard. He rattled off a number of constitutional provi-sions that, he said, would prevent a state from engaging in such blatant partisanship: "Establishment Clause, the Equal Protection Clause, Due Process Clause, other inde-pendent constitutional bars could apply." When pressed to explain how any of these would make a difference, Keller faltered, and Justice Scalia came to his rescue: "I think all you have to say is whatever prevents Texas . . . in all of its other activities . . . from saying 'vote Republican' also applies in the context of license plates." Grateful for the lifeline, Keller responded, "That's correct, Justice Scalia," and moved on to a more promising line of argument. The license plates represent government speech, he explained, and when the state speaks, it gets to decide what it will and will not say.

R. James George, the Sons' lawyer, countered that nobody regards license plates as government speech. When you drive behind a car with a specialty plate, you understand that it communicates the driver's view, not the state's. But the justices seemed unsettled by the implications of holding in the Sons' favor. If the state cannot refuse space to a Confederate flag, it cannot censor license plates at all. That means Lone Star State drivers could be treated to political messages like "make pot legal" and deeply offensive symbols like swastikas. In what may have been the funniest misheard question of the term, George thought Justice Ginsburg asked whether the word "vegan," truly an offensive term in red-meat-loving Texas, could appear on a license plate. She was asking about the word "jihad."

This line of questioning led Justice Antonin Scalia to remark to George that opening the floodgates would ultimately doom the whole enterprise: "You're really arguing for the abolition for Texas specialty plates, aren't you?"

In a 5–4 ruling on June 18, the thoroughly pragmatic Justice Breyer, joined by his liberal colleagues and—a rare ally—Justice Thomas, kept those floodgates shut tight. He held that messages on license plates are government speech, not private speech. States can say or refuse to say whatever they want without violating anyone's rights. The Sons' constitutional rights are not infringed, then, when Texas declines to publish its design.

Justice Breyer's rationale relied heavily on *Pleasant Grove City v. Summum*, a 2009 ruling permitting a city to decline a privately donated monument in a public park, even if it accepts other monuments from other private organizations. When monuments are erected in such a venue, they constitute government speech, the court held 9–0. The First Amendment is not offended when particular groups are denied the opportunity to express themselves with the city's stamp of approval.

License plates aren't quite like public monuments, Justice Breyer acknowledged, but they are similar enough to be adjudicated under the same standard. "When government speaks," he wrote, "it is not barred by the Free Speech Clause from determining the content of what it says." License plates have long "conveyed more than state names and vehicle identification numbers." They have also "communicated messages from the states" and various images (including a "Hereford steer" on the Arizona plate and the "Old Man of the Mountain" on the New Hampshire plate) since 1917. Idioms have a long and noble history as well. "Idaho Potatoes" came along in 1928; soon drivers were treated to "America's Dairyland" in Wisconsin and "Keep Florida Green."

Justice Breyer explained that Texas jumped on the bandwagon: "[T]he Texas Legislature has specifically authorized specialty plate designs stating, among other things, 'Read to Succeed,' 'Houston Livestock Show and Rodeo,' 'Texans Conquer Cancer,' and 'Girl Scouts.'" When the state prints license plates, the "governmental nature" of the message is right there in black and white. "The state places the name 'TEXAS' in large letters at the top of every plate," making them "essentially, government IDs."

Justice Alito found this argument laughably weak. He must have had a ball writing this devastating response:

> Here is a test. Suppose you sat by the side of a Texas highway and studied the license plates on the vehicles passing by . . . If a car with a plate that says "Rather Be

Golfing" passed by at 8:30 am on a Monday morning, would you think: "This is the official policy of the State— better to golf than to work?" If you did your viewing at the start of the college football season and you saw Texas plates with the names of the University of Texas's out-of-state competitors in upcoming games—Notre Dame, Oklahoma State, the University of Oklahoma, Kansas State, Iowa State—would you assume that the state of Texas was officially (and perhaps treasonously) rooting for the Longhorns' opponents?

Justice Breyer did not attempt to respond to this critique. He just left it aside. That might be because he acknowledged its strength. No reasonable Texas driver would interpret his state as cheering for nearby states' football teams. No reasonable Texas driver would conclude that the state of Texas would, itself, "Rather Be Golfing." And no reasonable Texas driver would see "Dr. Pepper: Always One of a Kind" or "Mighty Fine Burgers," or any of the other 350 available plate designs, and infer that Texas endorses particular soft drinks or fast-food establishments. To think of license plate designs as "government speech" is to twist the concept a bit out of shape.

All these messages on Texas license plates are best construed as miniature paid advertisements, as Justice Alito observed in his dissent. Drivers shell out an extra fee for the privilege of broadcasting messages on their trunk lids. "States have not adopted specialty license plate programs like Texas's because they are now bursting with things they want to say on their license plates," Justice Alito wrote. "Those programs were adopted because they bring in money." The Texas license plate program, in

Justice Alito's eyes, "sells . . . space to those who wish to
use it to express a personal message—provided only that
the message does not express a viewpoint that the State
finds unacceptable. That is not government speech; it is
the regulation of private speech."

Justice Breyer's opinion in support of Texas's right
to deny space to the Confederate flag made hardly any
mention of the racist semiotics of the design. The deeply
problematic and offensive meaning of the flag was officially just a side point, though it probably did more work
in motivating the decision than in supplying its rationale.
The question now is whether Justice Alito is right to worry
that *Sons of Confederate Veterans* greases a slippery slope
toward increased government regulation of viewpoints
it doesn't like. What if the court has unwittingly invited
states to censor private speech by co-opting it as government expression and then clamping down on what people
can say in parks, town squares, or city hall? In reality, this
risk is minimal. As dubious as Justice Kennedy's move
was in *Walker* to strip individual expression out of license
plate designs, it would be preposterous to argue that what
people say or the signs they hold up in public spaces are
really government speech. So, as Justice Breyer said in the
oral argument, the ruling for Texas poses "little harm to
speech." There are always bumper stickers.

Williams-Yulee v. Florida Bar

Since she retired from the Supreme Court in 2006,
Justice Sandra Day O'Connor has embarked on a campaign against a practice used in thirty-nine states: the

election of judges. "Courts are the bulwark of our society," she has said. "We cannot afford to have them undermined" by perceptions of illegitimacy. When potential judges are forced to campaign for seats on the bench and to raise money for those campaigns, unsavory results can ensue. Florida is a case in point, a state where judges have a poor reputation for honesty and fairness and where, in the 1970s, outrageous corruption scandals led four justices of the state's highest court to resign. An amicus brief in this term's *Williams-Yulee v. Florida Bar* submitted by a dozen Florida jurists and lawyers explains the context: "Several justices attempted to fix cases on behalf of campaign supporters. Another justice resigned after he was filmed on a gambling junket to Las Vegas paid for by a dog track that had a case pending before the high court, while others allowed themselves to be lobbied by a lawyer representing the public utilities industry in a case with major implications to the rate-paying public and even permitted him to ghostwrite the opinion for the Florida Supreme Court."

In an attempt to shore up the legitimacy of its courts, Florida adopted a Code of Judicial Ethics in 1994. In Canon 7C(1) of this code, candidates for judicial office are barred from "personally solicit[ing] campaign funds, or solicit[ing] attorneys for publicly stated support." Fifteen years later, Lanell Williams-Yulee broke this rule when she signed a letter requesting contributions for her 2009 campaign to become Hillsborough County judge. "I want to bring fresh ideas and positive solutions to the Judicial bench," she wrote, followed by a request for cash. Rebuked publicly and slapped with a $1,860.30 fine, Williams-Yulee fought back, claiming she had a First Amendment right to solicit campaign funds in her own name. Her free-speech

Chapter 2

suit was unsuccessful in the Florida Supreme Court, and she filed a petition for certiorari at the United States Supreme Court. It was granted.

"Whether state court judges should be chosen through election or appointment is the subject of vigorous debate in our country," Williams-Yulee's brief to the justices began, but "under our Constitution, 'States are free to choose [elections] rather than . . . appointment and confirmation' as the method that will 'select those persons likely to achieve judicial excellence.'" Quoting a 2003 case penned by Justice Anthony Kennedy, the brief noted that "[t]he State cannot opt for an elected judiciary and then assert that its democracy, in order to work as desired, compels the abridgement of speech." This contention seemed to bend the justices' ears during the oral argument, held on January 15, 2015. The conservative justices kept coming back to the idea that once a state decides to elect its judges, it cannot try to scale back the popular nature of elections by imposing unconstitutional restrictions on candidates' speech. "The fundamental choice was made by the State when they said we're going to have judges elected," Chief Justice Roberts noted.

Williams-Yulee's lawyer, Andrew Pincus, claimed that Canon 7C(1) is both *underinclusive* and *overinclusive:* given the aims of the ethical code, it bans too little speech, and it curtails some expression without good cause. Pincus met with the greatest success in pressing the first point. There are many ways, he reminded the justices, that Florida permits judicial candidates to raise money for their campaigns. The ethical code allows them to send out solicitation letters through the proxy of a campaign chairman, to see a list of the donors and how much they gave, and to compose personal thank-you notes to supporters after they have written checks to the campaign. There remains ample room, then, for perceptions of quid-pro-quo shenanigans even if the judicial candidate is prohibited from signing her name to the solicitation letter. The judicial ethics code bans a narrow slice of speech when—to really sever the link between "quid" and "quo"—it would need to ban much more.

Several justices on the court's liberal wing tried to show that keeping the judicial candidate's name off the letter makes a real difference. Justice Sonia Sotomayor noted the pressure that personal appeals can put on lawyers likely to be arguing cases before a judge on the ballot: "It's very, very, very rare that either by letter or by personal call that I ask a lawyer to do something . . . that that lawyer will say no. Isn't it inherent in the lawyer-judge context that people are going to say yes?"

Justice Stephen Breyer echoed this sentiment, making Florida's case with greater clarity and force than did Barry Richard, Florida's lawyer. It is "almost universal," Justice Breyer said, that lawyers pony up when asked for campaign contributions from judges. "It's not just confidence in the judiciary, is it? I mean, for a judge to ask for a quid puts pressure on people to give it. And that is a different evil than their simply knowing what happens, and I would say probably worse. To send a thank-you note is a form of politeness that creates knowledge, but does not to the same degree put pressure on the person to contribute."

Though Florida's position was supported by fourteen amicus briefs, to the petitioner's four, Richard never got much grip on his argument. Chief Justice Roberts observed near the end of the hearing that Richard faced a "great burden in trying to figure out how you're going to fix [elections] without contravening the First Amendment." Richard agreed the burden was great. He had to show that the rule against personal solicitation brings significant benefits in reducing judicial corruption—otherwise, the rule's limitation on speech would not be justified. But at the same time, Richard maintained that the rule is not "so Draconian that the person could not raise enough money to reasonably be able to broadcast the message." There is "no imposition, appreciably," Richard said, "on a candidate's expressive ability." In other words, the rule is absolutely necessary, but the judge will hardly notice it.

The skeptical tenor of the chief justice's questions led most observers to predict he would join his conservative brethren to issue a 5–4 win for Williams-Yulee. So it was a big surprise when, the day after the historic same-sex marriage cases were argued, the chief announced he was siding with the liberals and voting to uphold Canon 7C(1) against the First Amendment challenge. The last time Chief Justice Roberts had joined the court's liberal quartet against the four conservatives was in 2012, when he stunned everyone by writing the opinion upholding the individual mandate of the Affordable Care Act in *National Federation of Independent Business v. Sebelius.* Then, as now, the public's perception of the courts—and the Supreme Court in particular—seemed foremost in his mind.

The chief justice opened his majority opinion in *Williams-Yulee* by noting a distinction between judges and other elected officials: "Judges are not politicians, even when they come to the bench by way of the ballot. And a State's decision to elect its judiciary does not compel it to treat judicial candidates like campaigners for political office. A State may assure its people that judges will apply the law without fear or favor—and without having personally asked anyone for money." In a wide-ranging opinion, Chief Justice Roberts veered from the Middle Ages ("[t]o no one will we sell, to no one will we refuse or delay, right or justice," reads the Magna Carta of 1215) to twenty-first-century school girls ("[t]he identity of the solicitor matters, as anyone who has encountered a Girl Scout selling cookies outside a grocery store can attest"). He argued that the Florida ethics rule passes strict scrutiny: avoiding the perception of impropriety in the administration of justice is a compelling goal, and banning personal solicitation by judicial candidates is a narrowly tailored strategy for advancing it.

The four conservative justices penned three scathing dissents, including one from Justice Anthony Kennedy noting the "irony" that judicial candidates would have their own First Amendment rights curtailed before they even took the bench to protect those rights for others. Justice Antonin Scalia wrote that the majority upheld the ethics rule through a "sleight of hand" and "twistifications." Justice Samuel Alito called Canon 7C(1) "about as narrowly tailored as a burlap bag."

The level of rancor emanating from colleagues who are usually Chief Justice Roberts's jurisprudential friends was a sight to behold. But the practical implications of the *Williams-Yulee* decision are quite unlikely to measure up to the billing some gave it on the day it came down: "Campaign finance reformers just won a massive victory at the Supreme Court," Andrew Prokop rah-rahed in his headline at *Vox*. Surprising result, yes. But a "massive victory" for campaign finance reform? Probably not. As the majority opinion notes in response to Justice Kennedy's overzealous dissent, "Canon 7C(1) restricts a narrow slice of speech." The ethics rule leaves candidates for judgeships free to "contact potential supporters in person, on the phone, or online. They can promote their campaigns on radio, television, or other media." And judicial candidates can "direct their campaign committees" to raise money on their behalf.

So as Garrett Epps wrote at *The Atlantic*, *Williams-Yulee* is a "narrow and self-limited win for campaign-finance reform," not a decision presaging the rollback of *Citizens United v. FEC*, the Supreme Court's hugely controversial 2010 decision that unleashed unlimited outside spending on political campaigns. In fact, as First Amendment lion Floyd Abrams wrote, "critics of *Citizens United* can take no solace" from this decision. *Williams-Yulee* is "rooted in all respects in the difference between judicial elections and all others. If anything, the more the court focuses on the special and distinct role of judges as opposed to other elected officials, the more firmly it reinforces its earlier ruling as to the latter."

Three years ago, when Roberts voted with the court's four liberals to save the Affordable Care Act in *NFIB v. Sebelius*, he avoided what would have been seen by the public as party-line voting undermining President Obama's signature legislative achievement. He came to Obamacare's rescue a second time this year in *King v. Burwell*. And the chief's majority opinion in Williams-Yulee is another reflection of his commitment to cultivate the appearance of fair-mindedness and impartiality in America's judiciary, including and especially in its highest court.

Hugo Black, who served on the Supreme Court from 1937 to 1971, once wrote that freedom of expression is "wholly 'beyond the reach' of federal power to abridge." But even free-speech "absolutists" like Justice Black acknowledge that there are some legitimate constraints that the government may put on expression. The justices have enormous challenges in articulating which constraints are legitimate, and in previous terms, the Roberts court erred very much on the side of protecting speech. In the three free-expression cases analyzed in this chapter, we find a 1-2 split: once (in *Elonis*) the justices sided with the speaker (although, as explained previously, not because he had a First Amendment right to publish those violent posts) and twice (*Williams-Yulee* and *Sons of Confederate Veterans*) they upheld limitations on speech. Candidates for judicial office can be stopped from soliciting campaign funds from potential donors, and states can refuse to broadcast any and all messages on their license plates, but abusive ex-husbands on the Internet cannot be jailed unless it can be shown that they had some level of intent to threaten their estranged wives. The casual observer could be forgiven for finding that particular array of decisions a trifle curious. But as Justice Stephen Breyer noted in his brief concurrence in *Williams-Yulee,* it is naive to put too much stock in the "levels of scrutiny" judges employ to evaluate whether a particular restriction on speech contravenes the First Amendment. These levels are "guides" rather than rigid standards, he wrote. And they, like the court's precedents, are pliable tools in the hands of judges with myriad motivations.

Chapter 3

The Right to Privacy:
Police Latitude in Traffic Stops

Heien v. North Carolina; Rodriguez v. United States

The Supreme Court saw an unusual degree of drama during October Term 2014, but measured in terms of public outcry, the most dramatic legal news of the year took place outside the Washington Beltway. In Ferguson, Missouri, and on Staten Island in New York City, a pair of grand juries decided not to indict police officers who had killed unarmed African American men in the course of confrontations over petty crimes. The shooting of eighteen-year-old Michael Brown (who had stolen several cigarillos from a convenience store and pushed the clerk) and the illegal chokehold that led to the death of forty-three-year-old Eric Garner (suspected of selling single cigarettes, or "loosies") sparked protests in both communities. Those demonstrations widened and grew in urgency following the announcement that neither of the police officers would face a trial. Railing against perceived police brutality, protesters chanted, "No Justice, No Peace," "Black Lives Matter," and, echoing Eric Garner's words as officer

Daniel Pantaleo squeezed his neck while Garner writhed on the sidewalk, "I Can't Breathe."

The protests reached a new height in late April when, on the eve of the Supreme Court's hearing in the same-sex marriage case, riots erupted in Baltimore in the wake of the death of Freddie Gray, an unarmed twenty-five-year-old African American man who fell into a coma after being handled with indiscriminate force by six police officers. The violent protests reduced Baltimore to chaos, with more than 250 arrests, 20 injured police officers, and the declaration of a state of emergency. In contrast to the Ferguson and Staten Island cases, though, the officers will face criminal charges. Gray's death was declared a homicide by the medical examiner.

And two weeks after the October Term 2014 ended, Sandra Bland, a twenty-eight-year-old black woman, was pulled over by an aggressive police officer in Texas for failing to signal when changing lanes. She was found dead in her jail cell three days later after an apparent suicide.

The justices did not weigh in on any of these tragic episodes. They were local matters. A federal civil rights investigation by the Department of Justice into the Ferguson police department yielded no indictment of Darren Wilson, the officer who killed Michael Brown. Yet the shadows of Ferguson and Staten Island hovered over two Supreme Court cases asking how much leeway police should have in routine traffic stops.

Both cases to reach the high court inquired into the meaning of the Fourth Amendment "right of the people to be secure in their persons, houses, papers, and effects, against unreasonable searches and seizures." This is one of the most frequently litigated phrases in the Bill of Rights and one of the most familiar to fans of television dramas like *Law and Order*. People have less privacy when driving on public streets than they do when relaxing in their living rooms, the Supreme Court has held. Drivers can be stopped and checked for sobriety (*Michigan Dept. of State Police v. Sitz,* 1990), for example, and a motorist who has been lawfully arrested and poses a threat to police officers or could tamper with evidence of a crime is subject to a search of the passenger area of the car without a warrant (*Arizona v. Gant,* 2008). But while your car isn't quite your castle, the Constitution still protects you from general automotive searches in most circumstances.

Heien v. North Carolina

The facts in *Heien v. North Carolina,* the first case argued in October Term 2014, trace back to April 29, 2009. That morning, Matt Darisse, a sergeant of the Surry County Sheriff's Department, sat on the side of the road watching traffic head north on Interstate 77. Around 8:00 a.m., his suspicions were aroused by a slow-moving Ford Escort whose driver appeared "very stiff and nervous." Sergeant Darisse began following the Escort and, when he noticed a few miles up the road that it had a broken right brake light, pulled it over. Peering into the Escort and puzzling over a man lying across the back seat, Darisse asked the driver (Maynor Javier Vasquez) and the passenger (Nicholas Heien) where they were headed. Vasquez said West Virginia; Heien said Kentucky. Increasingly suspicious of the men, Darisse secured Heien's assent to search his car.

Darisse then found a stash of cocaine in a duffle bag and arrested Heien on attempted drug trafficking charges.

Heien invited this trouble when he let Darisse search his Escort: without evidence of any crime under way and just a gut feeling that something was amiss, the sergeant had no legal basis for an unconsented search. Heien would have been wise to refuse the officer's request. But after he had consented to the search and the drugs were discovered, Heien was charged with attempted cocaine trafficking. Heien then moved to suppress the evidence on the grounds that the stop and search were unconstitutional under the Fourth Amendment.

At trial, the suppression motion was denied. The jury found that the nonworking brake light gave the sergeant reasonable suspicion to pull Heien over and that the ensuing search was valid because Heien had agreed to it. Heien then pleaded guilty but did not give up his right to appeal the decision regarding the suppression of the cocaine.

This was Heien's first wise move. On appeal, the North Carolina Court of Appeals reversed his conviction on the grounds that it is not required to have two working brake lights when driving in the Tar Heel State. The law just requires the light to be functional on one side or the other. This means the officer's original decision to pull over the suspiciously steered Escort was based on a legal misapprehension. The error of law made the stop "objectively unreasonable," and the evidence collected at the scene may not be used against the motorist.

The issue before the Supreme Court was whether, in fact, Darisse's mistake made the stop "unreasonable" and therefore unconstitutional. If it was, the drugs seized on the shoulder of Interstate 77 should not have been used as evidence against Heien in the first place.

On December 15, 2014, by a vote of 8–1, the court decided in favor of the state. In reaching the conclusion that the officer was in error but not *unreasonably* so, the court majority cited a line from *Riley v. California*, a cell-phone-search case decided in 2014, that "the ultimate touchstone of the Fourth Amendment is 'reasonableness.'" Both the text of the Constitution and the history of its interpretation by the justices bears this out. But what does "reasonable" mean? It must mean more than simply "having a reason," as police officers may be said to have a reason to, say, racially profile drivers. The concept instead means having a *good* reason, or at least a *permissible* reason. And this is where things get hazy.

The key line from the *Heien* majority decision was this: "To be reasonable is not to be perfect, and so the Fourth Amendment allows for some mistakes on the part of government officials, giving them 'fair leeway for enforcing the law in the community's protection.'"

On first blush, this sounds plausible. One can understand why Darisse might have misconstrued North Carolina law on this point. But pause a moment, and one begins to wonder how much leeway is "fair." How error prone can an officer be before his bungled policing crosses a line?

It is a well-known principle that ignorance is no excuse for breaking a law. If you turn right on a red light in New York City, even after coming to a complete stop, the police will hand you a ticket bearing a $100 to $300 fine. It's no excuse to say it's your first day in the big city and that right turns on red are permitted everywhere else you've ever driven. No: you need to know the law, and you need to follow it. So why did eight justices say it's all right for police officers to make "reasonable" mistakes about the law they are purportedly enforcing? Here is the chief justice's reasoning:

> Heien and *amici* point to the well-known maxim, "Ignorance of the law is no excuse," and contend that it is fundamentally unfair to let police officers get away with mistakes of law when the citizenry is accorded no such leeway. Though this argument has a certain rhetorical appeal, it misconceives the implication of the maxim. The true symmetry is this: Just as an individual generally cannot escape criminal liability based on a mistaken understanding of the law, so too the government cannot impose criminal liability based on a mistaken understanding of the law. If the law required two working brake lights, Heien could not escape a ticket by claiming he reasonably thought he needed only one; if the law required only one, Sergeant Darisse could not issue a valid ticket by claiming he reasonably thought drivers needed two. But just because mistakes of law cannot justify either the imposition or the avoidance of criminal liability, it does not follow that they cannot justify an investigatory stop. And Heien is not appealing a brake-light ticket; he is appealing a cocaine-trafficking conviction.

In other words, you *can* be thrown in a jail for a police officer's misunderstanding of the law if the mistake has nothing to do with the crime the mistake helped reveal. Justice Sotomayor laid into what she perceived as the majority's spongy assurances that "the mistakes must be those of reasonable men." Without directly referring to the episodes of deadly policing in Ferguson and New York City, Justice Sotomayor alluded to the exact concerns underlying the protests: "[W]hen an officer acts on pretext, at least that pretext would be the violation of an actual law . . . Giving officers license to effect seizures so long as they can attach to their reasonable view of the facts some reasonable legal interpretation (or misinterpretation) that suggests a law has been violated significantly expands this authority . . . *One wonders how a citizen seeking to be law-abiding and to structure his or her behavior to avoid these invasive, frightening, and humiliating encounters could do so*" (emphasis added).

Notice that Justice Sotomayor had no trouble with the mismatch between Darisse's real concern about the Escort (the "very stiff and nervous" look on the driver's face) and the broken taillight, his pretext for pulling the driver over. This policing tactic is common and perfectly legal. An officer can't (officially) pull you over for looking suspicious, but he can stop you for failing to signal when changing lanes or for rolling through a stop sign. Even the petitioner raises no hackles at the pretextual nature of his traffic stop. In his brief to the justices, Heien does not "contest the legality of this practice." But he does insist that "limitations exist on officers' ability to use wholly innocent conduct on this Nation's roadways as justification for seizing individuals to investigate inarticulable suspicions of impropriety."

Two of the court's liberal justices joined the majority with some misgivings. In a concurring opinion, Elena Kagan and Ruth Bader Ginsburg warned that while the majority interpreted Darisse's mistake as a reasonable one, other officers in other cases should not assume that their flubs are excusable. It all depends: "If the statute is genuinely ambiguous, such that overturning the officer's judgment requires hard interpretive work, then the officer has made a reasonable mistake. But if not, not."

So for Justices Kagan and Ginsburg, if a police officer makes a mistake based on a faulty interpretation of an *unambiguous* law, the evidence collected during his traffic stop cannot, under the Fourth Amendment, be the basis of a prosecution. But who is to say how ambiguous the law really is, or how "reasonable" the officer's mistake might be? This does seem, as Justice Sotomayor observes in her dissent, to be an untenable basis for affording the Fourth Amendment a stable, ascertainable meaning. A sliding scale of reasonability depending on the relative ambiguity of the law in question "will prove murky in application," she wrote: "[T]he Court's unwillingness to sketch a fuller view of what makes a mistake of law reasonable only presages the likely difficulty that courts will have applying the court's decision in this case."

Rodriguez v. United States

A month after the court released its decision in *Heien*, it revisited the Fourth Amendment in *Rodriguez v. United States,* a case concerning the constitutionality of a late-night drug-detecting dog sniff that took place on the shoulder of a Nebraska state highway in 2012. Dennys Rodriguez, the driver of a Mercury Mountaineer, and Scott Pollman, the passenger, were pulled over for slightly veering off the roadway. The police officer, Morgan

Struble, didn't buy Rodriguez's line that he swerved to avoid a pothole or Pollman's explanation that they were driving back to Norfolk, Nebraska, from Omaha, where they had looked into buying a Ford Mustang. When he asked Rodriguez to come sit in the patrol car with him while he completed some paperwork, Struble found it odd that the driver refused. In his experience, the police officer later testified, this refusal was a "subconscious behavior that people concealing contraband will exhibit."

Struble had the idea of taking his drug-detection dog on a walk around the car to sniff it out. Being alone and needing backup, he called for another officer to assist him. While they were waiting, Struble wrote a warning ticket to Rodriguez for driving on the shoulder and returned the driver's license and registration papers. The traffic stop was seemingly over at 12:25 a.m., but Struble did not consider the driver to be "free to leave." Eight minutes later, the backup patrol car arrived and, sure enough, after nosing around the Mercury, the dog smelled something. Officers searched the car and found a sizeable bag of methamphetamine, and Rodriguez was convicted on drug charges.

The Supreme Court's question in *Rodriguez* was whether the officer overstepped constitutional bounds by detaining the driver for an extra eight minutes before conducting the dog sniff. At the oral argument, most of the justices seemed untroubled by the delay. Justice Scalia and the chief justice both drew laughter when cheekily noting that they have not personally had the experience of being stopped by a police officer. "People have told me," Roberts said, that officers usually ask for "license and registration." Scalia joked, when asking how long it's "reasonable" to be detained on the side of the road, "I want to know what it is so I can complain when it's longer." But again, Justice Sotomayor stood up for the suspects. "Chief, I've been stopped," she began. "Keeping me past giving me the ticket is annoying as *heck* whether it's 5 minutes, 10 minutes, 45."

It may have been this personal, direct appeal to Roberts that gave him pause. Perhaps it was Justice Sotomayor's dissent in *Heien*. Or maybe the swirling news events about police abusing their power when apprehending people less privileged than John Roberts got the chief thinking. It may have been all of the above. But one thing is clear: when the Supreme Court issued its 6–3 opinion on April 21, 2015, both the chief justice and Justice Scalia had joined the court's liberals in finding the dog sniff unconstitutional under the Fourth Amendment.

In a crisp nine-page opinion, Justice Ginsburg applied a few precedents to find that the permissible length of traffic stops "is determined by the seizure's 'mission'—to address the traffic violation that warranted the stop." A police officer may detain a motorist only as long as is necessary to accomplish the primary mission of the stop. Once an officer has completed the task at hand, he may not prolong an investigation unless he has "reasonable suspicion" of further wrongdoing. "We hold," Justice Ginsburg concluded, "that a police stop exceeding the time needed to handle the matter for which the stop was made violates the Constitution's shield against unreasonable seizures."

In dissent, Justice Thomas pointed to the total elapsed time of Struble's stop: twenty-nine minutes. "That amount of time is hardly out of the ordinary for a traffic stop by a single officer of a vehicle containing multiple occupants even when no dog sniff is involved." The "touchstone of the Fourth Amendment is reasonableness" (as the court has held), and "reasonable" is defined according to "the totality of the circumstances." There is no sense, Justice Thomas argued, in which a half-hour traffic stop is beyond the pale of reasonable policing.

Justice Alito agreed, penning his own short dissent and arguing that *Rodriguez* is "unlikely to have any appreciable effect on the length of future traffic stops." When they are trained in the art of pulling people over, Justice Alito argued, police will "learn the prescribed sequence of events" that will keep them within the bounds of the Fourth Amendment while getting every piece of information they need. It may just be a matter of not handing over the traffic ticket until the dog has circumnavigated the car to the satisfaction of the officer.

With these cases stacked up against one another, we find a broadening of police latitude in traffic stops (*Heien*) abutting what seems to be a constraint on the same practice (*Rodriguez*). The counteracting vectors seem to amount to a slight overall expansion of privacy rights for drivers and a corresponding slight contraction of police power. But the implications of these split decisions won't ultimately be known until motorists turn to them in lawsuits complaining that police officers have unreasonably detained them on the nation's roads. It is an open question when an officer's ignorance of a traffic law is "reasonable" and when it isn't. And we won't know if Justice Alito is right about how easy it will be for cops to evade the new rule in *Rodriguez* until courts are called upon to apply Justice Ginsburg's holding. In the meantime, debates over police misbehavior on the streets of American cities show few signs of abating.

Chapter 4

Cruel and Unusual Punishment: Death Penalty Drugs

Glossip v. Gross

Three years after he wrote the opinion in *Roe v. Wade* that made early-term abortion a constitutional right, Justice Harry Blackmun came down on the conservative side of another life-or-death constitutional question. In 1976, he voted with the majority in *Gregg v. Georgia* to lift a four-year ban on capital punishment, permitting executions to start up again in the United States. But eighteen years later, on the cusp of retirement, the eighty-five-year-old justice changed his mind. In 1994, Justice Blackmun declared he would "no longer tinker with the machinery of death." Just a few months before he left the bench, Justice Blackmun reversed his previous view that capital punishment was consistent with the Eighth Amendment's ban on cruel and unusual punishment. "The death penalty experiment," he concluded, "has failed," and it is a "delusion" to think otherwise.

Justice Blackmun's prediction that the court would eventually reach this conclusion has not come to pass. Yet the United States is steadily marching away from the death penalty. Public support for executing murderers has fallen from a high of 80 percent in the mid-1990s to 63 percent today. The number of executions rose from thirty-one in 1994 to a peak of ninety-eight in 1999 and then began dropping as more and more states declared death penalty moratoria or abolished the ultimate penalty altogether. On May 20, 2015, Nebraska became the nineteenth state to abolish capital punishment and the first predominantly Republican state to do so in four decades.

In 2014, of the thirty-five people who were put to death in the United States, at least three died grisly, painful deaths. In April 2014, it took Clayton Lockett, an inmate in Oklahoma, forty-three minutes to die after writhing in pain. ("This shit is fucking with my head," he said, head bucking, before he finally died.) Three months later, Joseph Wood visibly suffered for more than ninety minutes before dying in a botched execution in Arizona.

On January 23, 2015, the Supreme Court agreed to hear *Glossip v. Gross,* a case challenging three pending executions in Oklahoma. The inmates contended that Oklahoma's lethal-injection protocol violates the Eighth Amendment by subjecting the condemned to a substantial risk of being tortured to death. When states began using lethal injection to execute criminals in the late 1970s, the hope was to make state killing more humane. This method worked without much drama for a couple of decades. But in recent years, a key drug in the execution cocktail, the one that knocks out the individual before two other drugs stop his breathing and his heart, has been hard to come by. This has led some of the thirty-one states that have the death penalty to improvise, with frightful results.

The drug in question in *Glossip v. Gross,* midazolam, had been adopted by Oklahoma and a few other states as a substitute for barbiturates like sodium thiopental and pentobarbital. Sources of these drugs, which reliably induce a coma-like state, dried up when European manufacturers with moral objections to capital punishment stopped supplying them to American prisons. Midazolam is a sedative, not a barbiturate. It is typically used to treat seizures and for sedation prior to certain surgical procedures like colonoscopies. It had never been used in an execution until 2013.

In an uncommonly tense and grim oral argument on April 29, 2015, the justices struggled to play scientist for a day in their effort to decide whether midazolam, when used in an execution cocktail, contravenes the Constitution. The lawyers presented conflicting medical claims. The attorney for the inmates, Robin Konrad, told the justices, "[T]his drug is not able to pharmacologically do what the State's expert said that it could in fact do." The suitability of midazolam in executions is "not supported by any scientific literature," she said. Moreover, it isn't possible to ensure a prisoner reaches unconsciousness by increasing the dosage: "Mr. Wood's execution demonstrates the ceiling effect," Konrad noted, "that giving more of this drug is not going to put a prisoner into a deep coma-like" state. So higher and higher dosages are not likely to make a difference.

Not to be deterred, Oklahoma's unflappable lawyer, Patrick Wyrick, chased down every question lobbed at him by the court's liberal justices in staking out his main contention: midazolam is, in fact, capable of inducing unconsciousness. In a very testy exchange with Justice

Sotomayor that earned her a not-so-subtle rebuke from the chief justice, Wyrick demonstrated a superior grasp of the issue. At one point, when Justice Sotomayor got deep in the weeds on the effects of midazolam, Wyrick told her, "respectfully, you have that backwards."

The most fiery moments in the hearing came when death penalty politics sneaked into the legal dilemma. "Let's be honest about what's going on here," said Justice Samuel Alito in a tone that was even crankier than usual, which is saying something. "Oklahoma and other states could carry out executions painlessly," he said, pointing to jurisdictions where assisted-suicide laws allow for a peaceful death. Yet the state has been boxed into a corner by a "guerrilla war against the death penalty." It would be inappropriate, he held, for the justices to "countenance" that war, "which consists of efforts to make it impossible for the states to obtain drugs that could be used to carry out capital punishment with little, if any pain."

Justice Antonin Scalia then chimed in, saying that more effective sedatives "have been rendered unavailable by the abolitionist movement putting pressure on the companies that manufacture them." Isn't that "relevant," he said, "to the decision that you're putting before us?" Konrad seemed taken aback by these questions. Though she gave what seems to be the correct answer—"I don't think that it's relevant"—she did not state it with much conviction. It doesn't matter, from the point of view of the Eighth Amendment, *why* a particular drug has come to be adopted by a state for its execution regimen. If that drug fails to do its job, if it gives prisoners the sensation of being burned alive, it is unconstitutional. Does the Constitution permit Konrad's three clients to endure a risk of being tortured to death because drug manufacturers—whether under pressure from death-penalty abolitionists or of their own accord—no longer supply drugs that kill criminals painlessly?

When the justices released their 5–4 decision on June 29, 2015, the politics of the death penalty played a starring role. Justice Alito penned the majority opinion for an angrily divided court, holding that the plaintiffs had not established that midazolam violates the Eighth Amendment. Oklahoma may go ahead and execute the prisoners by using midazolam as the first shot in a lethal three-drug cocktail, Justice Alito wrote, for "two independent reasons."

First, as long as the death penalty is constitutional (and it has been, for nearly forty years), there must be a constitutional method of carrying it out. If midazolam isn't sufficient to prevent the condemned from suffering during the execution, the burden is on the plaintiffs to show that a less painful alternative to midazolam is available. But "the prisoners failed to identify a known and available alternative method of execution that entails a lesser risk of pain, a requirement of all Eighth Amendment method-of-execution claims." Referring to *Baze v. Rees,* a 2008 decision upholding a four-drug lethal-injection regimen in Kentucky, Justice Alito noted that "prisoners must identify an alternative that is 'feasible, readily implemented, and in fact significantly reduce[s] a substantial risk of severe pain.'" While most of us "wish to die a painless death, many do not have that good fortune," Justice Alito wrote, rather chillingly. To hold for the plaintiffs on the ground that midazolam entails some risk of pain, without identifying a fallback execution method, "would effectively outlaw the death penalty altogether."

Second, Justice Alito explained, even if a preferable method of execution were available, the plaintiffs would still lose. Why? Because the original court "did not commit clear error when it found that the prisoners failed to establish that Oklahoma's use of a massive dose of midazolam in its execution protocol entails a substantial risk of severe pain." In other words, even if midazolam does cause suffering during some executions, the trial court was not *clearly* in error in deciding otherwise: there was enough reassuring testimony from Dr. Roswell Evans, the state's witness in the record, to the effect that midazolam works just fine. According to Dr. Evans, "[T]he proper administration of a 500-milligram dose of midazolam would make it 'a virtual certainty' that any individual would be 'at a sufficient level of unconsciousness to resist the noxious stimuli which could occur from application of the 2nd and 3rd drugs' used in the Oklahoma protocol."

Glossip produced two remarkable dissenting opinions. Justice Sotomayor's dissent, joined by Justices Breyer, Ginsburg, and Kagan, included a scathing review of the state's expert. Dr. Evans, she wrote, gave testimony that was "scientifically unsupported and implausible." He "cited no scholarly research in support of his opinions," relying instead on general overviews of the pharmacological effects of midazolam found on "the Web site www .drugs.com, and a 'Material Safety Data Sheet' produced by a midazolam manufacturer." Testimony from the prisoners' rival experts, considered alongside the horrific details of three botched executions, raised enough doubt about the reliability of midazolam's effectiveness as a sedative to show that the district court had erred.

Next, Justice Sotomayor took on Justice Alito's first contention. The majority's operative syllogism—that because the death penalty is constitutional, there must be a method of execution that is constitutional—is rather cold-blooded: "A method of execution that is intolerably painful—even to the point of being the chemical equivalent of burning alive—will, the court holds, be unconstitutional if, and only if, there is a 'known and available alternative' method of execution." But it should not be the prisoner's responsibility to instruct the state in the best way to carry out an execution. "Certainly," Justice Sotomayor wrote, "the condemned has no duty to devise or pick a constitutional instrument of his or her own death." It is a "mystery," she wrote, why the majority blame the lethal-injection conundrum on death-penalty abolitionists:

> Petitioners here had no part in creating the shortage of execution drugs; it is odd to punish them for the actions of pharmaceutical companies and others who seek to disassociate themselves from the death penalty—actions which are, of course, wholly lawful. Nor, certainly, should these rapidly changing circumstances give us any greater confidence that the execution methods ultimately selected will be sufficiently humane to satisfy the Eighth Amendment. Quite the contrary. The execution protocols States hurriedly devise as they scramble to locate new and untested drugs . . . are all the more likely to be cruel and unusual—presumably, these drugs would have been the States' first choice were they in fact more effective.

Chapter 4

Justice Breyer's surprising dissent, which attracted only one additional vote (that of Justice Ginsburg), summoned dozens of studies and offered a comprehensive critique of the way the death penalty is administered in the United States. Going beyond the issue of relying on a questionable drug to render an inmate insensate to searing pain, Justice Breyer lamented the path of "try[ing] to patch up the death penalty's legal wounds one at a time." He invited (in future cases) a "full briefing on a more basic question: whether the death penalty violates the Constitution." It does, he argued. Capital punishment is seriously unreliable, carries a risk of killing innocents, is arbitrary in application, entails long delays between sentencing and execution, and has been "abandoned" in more and more places.

Assuming the role of a piqued high school debater, Justice Scalia replied to Justice Breyer point by point, but not before mocking his efforts as "waving . . . a ream of the most recent abolitionist studies (a superabundant genre) as though they have discovered the lost folios of Shakespeare." Justice Scalia made the rare move of summarizing his concurrence from the bench and the rarer antic of apparently deviating from his prepared remarks to vent about the same-sex marriage decision reached a few days earlier. According to *Slate's* Dahlia Lithwick, the performance was "very odd." She writes that Justice Scalia began his statement this way: "'Last Friday five justices of this court took the issue' of same-sex marriage away from the voters based on their 'policy preferences' and then noted that today two justices sought to do that again, with the call to abolish the death penalty."

These are bitter disagreements over an issue that has bitterly divided Americans for decades. What's notable in *Glossip v. Gross* is how one specific question about a single drug used in a particular method of executing criminals turned into a 127-page free-for-all on the constitutionality and ethics of the death penalty and the extrajudicial political campaign to abolish it. As the death penalty dwindles as a punishment for murder in the United States but the punishment remains on the books in a majority of the states, the justices will continue to find themselves tinkering with the details of its rather gruesome machinery.

Racial Equality: Disparate Impact Survives

Texas Department of Housing and Community Affairs v. Inclusive Communities Project

Days after Martin Luther King Jr. was assassinated in 1968, Congress passed the Fair Housing Act (FHA) to combat discrimination faced by minorities in search of a home. The FHA prohibited landlords, real-estate agents, and mortgage lenders from considering race, color, religion, sex, or national origin in making loans, selling homes, or choosing tenants. In 1988, Congress added disability and family status to the list of factors that may not inform housing transactions.

The FHA has helped broaden housing access for disfavored groups. But forty-four years after the law took effect, a 2012 federal report issued a sobering assessment. While "blatant forms of discrimination" have seen a sharp decline, "there can be no question that the housing circumstances of whites and minorities differ substantially." Blacks, Hispanics, and Asians have a tougher time making an appointment for an in-person meeting with a real-estate broker and are shown fewer properties, making their housing search longer and most costly. They are at a disadvantage in the lending market. They face discrimination from many landlords.

Home buyers or renters who feel they have been discriminated against can turn to the Department of Housing and Urban Development (HUD), which offers an online complaint form. After investigating the complaint, HUD may then schedule a hearing. But it's one thing to ban discrimination and quite another to prove discriminatory treatment. A landlord who comes out and declares to an African American couple that he only rents to whites will bring a lawsuit on himself—and he will lose. But a savvier racist landlord will keep his bias under his hat. He'll find another reason, a pretext, to justify a business decision that was in fact based on purely discriminatory motives.

Without a "smoking gun"—typically, a statement from a property owner betraying his discriminatory motive—it can be very difficult to establish a violation of the FHA. But if the owner's racism could be demonstrated by suspicious patterns in his business dealings—if he never or very rarely rented out his apartments to blacks, say, despite having many African American applicants—the complaining party may have a better case. Such a pattern may qualify as a so-called "disparate impact"—an adverse effect on a protected class of people. A disparate impact can be shown by examining the *results* of a series of decisions rather than by proving that the real-estate agent, seller, or lender had a *motive* to discriminate when he made those decisions. The FHA has been interpreted by nine federal appellate courts to permit the consideration of adverse effects in establishing liability. But in *Texas Department of Housing and Community Affairs v. Inclusive Communities Project*, the justices agreed to take up what seemed to be a long-settled question: Does the Fair Housing Act permit lawsuits based on the disparate impact understanding of racial equality?

The matter had narrowly missed coming to the Supreme Court twice before in the previous three years. To the relief of those who worried that the justices would vote to weaken protections under the FHA, both lawsuits were settled out of court before the justices met to hear arguments. On January 21, 2015, with civil rights organizations holding their collective breath, the issue finally came under the justices' consideration. The lawsuit arose in opposition to the manner in which Texas handed out tax credits to developers of apartment blocks for low-income people. From 1995 to 2009, the Texas Department of Housing and Community Affairs gave no credits to build affordable homes in the white suburbs of Dallas; it backed development only in inner-city neighborhoods populated by racial minorities. The Inclusive Communities Project (ICP), a Dallas nonprofit organization devoted to cultivating racial and economic integration, charged in its brief to the justices that by adhering to a color line in its tax credit allocations, Texas was propagating "ghetto conditions" in clear violation of the FHA.

In the lower courts, the ICP prevailed at both the trial and appellate levels. Using statistical analysis, the ICP convinced both courts that it had a prima facie case against Texas based on how the state allocated the tax credits. Under a legal standard established by the Second Circuit Court of Appeals in 2010, after demonstrating a disparate impact, the burden shifted to Texas to show that (1) it had a compelling governmental interest behind its decision to allocate tax credits for developments in predominantly minority neighborhoods and (2) there was no alternative way to pursue that interest that would have resulted in a less-discriminatory outcome. This is quite a demanding standard, and both the district court and Fifth Circuit Court of Appeals determined that Texas did not satisfy it.

The specific facts of the case were not much on the justices' minds during the oral hearing. Instead, they grappled with the wider question of whether the FHA bars only intentional discrimination or also targets practices that create a disparate impact on minorities. The lawyer for Texas, Scott Keller, kept directing the justices to read the law. "[I]ts plain text," he said repeatedly, in contrast to the wording of other civil rights laws, "doesn't use effects- or results-based language." The Texas housing department did not intentionally shut minorities out of white neighborhoods, in other words, so it is not subject to a discrimination complaint under the FHA.

Here Justice Antonin Scalia registered a surprising concern. Justice Scalia has held the concept of disparate impact in disdain for years. In a 2009 case regarding Title VII of the Civil Rights Act (which every justice except Clarence Thomas reads as permitting lawsuits based on disparate-impact liability), Scalia penned a concurrence warning of an "evil day" of reckoning when the court would have to decide whether the "disparate impact provisions of Title VII of the Civil Rights Act of 1964 [are] consistent with the Constitution's guarantee of equal protection" in the Fourteenth Amendment. In that case, *Ricci v. DeStefano,* Scalia strongly implied the answer is no, since avoiding discriminatory results would often require the state to "put a racial thumb on the scales" and "to make decisions based on (because of) those racial outcomes." So it raised eyebrows in the courtroom when Scalia asked Keller why Congress would have carved out three liability exceptions under the FHA in 1988 if it didn't believe the law recognized disparate impacts in the first place. "Why doesn't that kill your case?" he asked Keller. Here was the court's leading conservative voice on race suggesting that the Fair Housing Act may indeed allow complaints based on a showing of discriminatory effect.

It was a long half-hour for Keller. Michael Daniel, arguing against the Texas agency, didn't fare much better. "Racial disparity is not racial discrimination," scolded Justice Scalia, switching back to his standard line. "The fact that the NFL is largely black players is not discrimination." Solicitor General Donald Verrilli, defending the disparate-impact reading of the FHA but hedging on the merits of the Texas matter, encouraged the justices not to, in Justice Stephen Breyer's words, "throw the whole baby out" with the bathwater. Verrilli said that the FHA has, "for 35 or 40 years," smoked out supposedly neutral zoning or occupancy regulations that in fact have the effect of "excluding minorities." Texas responded that race was nowhere on its mind when handing out tax credits: developers opted to build subsidized homes in poorer neighborhoods because land is cheaper there and the new housing units would have a friendlier reception by locals.

In one of the biggest surprises of the term, the Supreme Court refused, by a 5–4 vote, to narrow the protections for racial minorities under the FHA. Little could be deduced from the two questions Justice Kennedy asked during the oral argument, but the opening paragraphs of his ruling quickly clarified where he stood. "The underlying dispute in this case," the opinion began, "concerns where housing for low-income persons should be constructed in Dallas, Texas—that is, whether the housing should be built in the inner city or in the suburbs."

The opinion observed that "vestiges" of "residential segregation by race" remain nearly one hundred years after housing segregation was declared unconstitutional in the 1917 case *Buchanan v. Warley.* Blacks and other minorities were left behind in dense urban centers as whites fled to the suburbs in the middle of the twentieth century. Other forces conspired to propagate *de facto* segregation even after legal (or *de jure*) segregation was a thing of the past: "Racially restrictive covenants prevented the conveyance of property to minorities . . . ; steering by real-estate agents led potential buyers to consider homes in racially homogenous areas; and discriminatory lending practices, often referred to as redlining, precluded minority families from purchasing homes in affluent areas."

Justice Kennedy then sketched the statutory context of the FHA, considering the law in light of litigation over two other antidiscrimination statutes that have been interpreted to countenance disparate impact: Title VII of the Civil Rights Act of 1964 and the Age Discrimination in Employment Act (ADEA), passed in 1967. In 1971, in *Griggs v. Duke Power Co.,* the Supreme Court found that it is illegal under Title VII for an employer to adopt a policy that adversely affects disadvantaged racial groups, even if no proof of a racist motive exists. The justices held unanimously that a high school graduation requirement for manual laborers had the impermissible effect of excluding racial minorities, with no "manifest relationship" between that requirement and the nature of the duties to be performed. And in the 2005 case *Smith v. City of Jackson,* the court found disparate impact implied in the ADEA's prohibition on age discrimination. Here too, the court held, unless a good reason can be proffered for giving more lucrative benefits to younger workers, an employer can be found liable for discriminating against older ones—even if he did not intend to treat them unfairly.

After examining these two cases, Justice Kennedy concluded that "antidiscrimination laws must be construed to encompass disparate-impact claims when their text refers to the consequences of actions and not just to the mindset of actors." The FHA, Justice Kennedy found, has considerations of consequences baked into section 804(a). It is illegal, the law reads, "to refuse to sell or rent after the making of a bona fide offer, or to refuse to negotiate for the sale or rental of, *or otherwise make unavailable* or deny, a dwelling to any person because of race, color, religion, sex, familial status, or national origin" (emphasis added).

Though the textual hook for disparate-impact claims in the FHA is the clause "otherwise make available" rather than "otherwise adversely affect" (as in Title VII and the ADEA), the meaning is basically the same, Justice Kennedy argued. Whether by design or not, housing policies causing disproportionate harm to blacks and other minorities are illegal under the FHA. Beyond the text, there are strong clues that Congress meant to permit disparate-impact claims. In 1988, lawmakers passed several amendments to the FHA that seemed to carve out exemptions to disparate-impact liability—implying strongly that the law countenances at least some disparate-impact claims. All nine courts of appeals to have taken up the FHA had recognized disparate-impact liability in the law; if Congress considered that a faulty interpretation, it could have clarified the statute in its amendments rather than given the disparate-impact reading an implicit stamp of approval.

Justice Kennedy was quick to put limits on this principle, however. Developers and other potential defendants, he wrote, should be shielded from "abusive disparate-impact claims." Plaintiffs need to show more than just statistical disparities to sue under the FHA, and a suit "must fail if the plaintiff cannot point to a defendant's policy or policies causing that disparity." Without such a requirement, defendants might be "held liable for racial disparities they did not create." And in seeking to avoid a racially disparate impact, lenders and real-estate agents should not go so far as to resort to disparate treatment of their clients that would run afoul of other provisions of Title VII and of the Fourteenth Amendment's equal protection clause— taking calls from mainly black applicants, for example, or giving them more favorable mortgage rates in an effort treat blacks fairly. With these caveats in mind, the court affirmed disparate-impact liability under the FHA and "acknowledge[d] the Fair Housing Act's continuing role in moving the Nation toward a more integrated society."

In his pistol-swinging, thirty-five-page dissent, Justice Alito aimed to shoot down every argument advanced in the majority opinion. He contended that neither the language of the FHA nor its legislative history "authorize[s] disparate-impact claims." He took issue with Justice Kennedy's reading of the court's precedents (in *Griggs* and *Smith*), which he characterized as "irreconcilable" with disparate-impact theory. He pooh-poohed the unanimity of the courts of appeals on the question: "While we always give respectful consideration to interpretations of statutes that garner wide acceptance in other courts, this Court has 'no warrant to ignore clear statutory language on the ground that other courts have done so,' even if they have 'consistently' done so for '30 years.'" Finally, while Justice Alito acknowledged that the purpose of the FHA is praise-worthy ("We agree that all Americans should be able 'to buy decent houses without discrimination . . . because of the color of their skin'"), he scolded the majority for overreaching: "[T]his Court has no license to expand the scope of the FHA to beyond what Congress enacted."

The court's decision, Justice Alito warned, will force a city to let rats run amok in apartment buildings. He cited a case in which St. Paul, Minnesota, permitted landlords to raise rents in order to provide residents with more reli-able responses to rodent infestations, among other provi-sions of the housing code. But since those rent increases fell mainly on racial minorities, they were found to con-stitute an illegal disparate impact. "Disparate impact puts housing authorities in a very difficult position," he wrote, "because programs that are designed and implemented to help the poor can provide the grounds for a disparate-impact claim." In sum, Justice Alito wrote, "the Court . . . makes a serious mistake" that will bring "unfortunate con-sequences for local government, private enterprise, and those living in poverty."

Despite the surprise of the decision in *Texas v. ICP*, it is a mistake to characterize it as a huge liberal victory. The 5–4 ruling, after all, simply leaves the Fair Housing Act alone. In an episode of narrowly averted conservative judicial activism, Justice Kennedy joined the court's liber-als to keep the civil rights law chugging along in just about the way it has been operating for decades. But it is unclear how the stipulations Justice Kennedy put on the operation of disparate-impact theory will affect the legal status of the precise issue at stake in the case: whether the Texas Department of Housing and Community Affairs erred in handing out contracts to housing developers. That question is now back in the hands of the lower court.

The Right to Vote: Race, Democracy, and Redistricting

Alabama Legislative Black Caucus v. Alabama;
Arizona State Legislature v. Arizona Independent
Redistricting Commission

It is an ironic feature of the American constitutional system that the nine members of the Supreme Court, the most powerful unelected officials in the federal government, have so much influence on American elections. The justices are regularly called upon to weigh in on voting rights and the drawing of legislative district lines, the highly politicized process known as "gerrymandering" that corrals voters into often oddly shaped districts where they have little chance of unseating incumbents.

The bedrock democratic principle of "one person, one vote," surprisingly, is nowhere to be found in the text of the Constitution. It took a 1964 Supreme Court ruling (*Reynolds v. Sims*) to announce that state and congressional district lines must to be drawn in such a way that voters' influence does not vary significantly based on where they live. In *Reynolds*, the justices chastised Alabama for huge population disparities in its state legislative districts:

in densely packed Jefferson County, six hundred thousand voters were represented by one senator and seven representatives (for a ratio of eighty-five thousand voters to one lawmaker), while districts with as few as fifteen thousand voters had one senator and one representative. Doing the math, this meant that a voter in Birmingham, the state's largest city, had about one-fifth of the voting power of a rural Alabamian. To correct this imbalance, deemed a violation of the Fourteenth Amendment's equal protection clause, the justices required Alabama to reapportion its voters into districts of roughly equal population.

During October Term 2014, the court refused to hear emergency petitions challenging new GOP-sponsored laws in Texas and Wisconsin requiring voters to show identification when entering polling places. Opponents of these laws say their purported purpose—deterring voter fraud—is a red herring. The real motivation behind voter ID laws is to keep minorities and the poor away from the polls, Democrats say, and in October 2014, Justice Ginsburg issued a rare, scathing six-page dissent (joined by Justices Kagan and Sotomayor) charging that the court's denial of review in the Texas case "may prevent more than 600,000 registered Texas voters (about 4.5 percent of all registered voters) from voting in person for lack of compliant identification."

The justices did, however, take up two key cases involving voting and elections. In *Alabama Legislative Black Caucus v. Alabama,* the court asked what role racial considerations may play in drawing up district maps. And in *Arizona State Legislature v. Arizona Independent Redistricting Commission,* it considered whether voters could tackle partisanship in map-drawing for Congress by taking the job out of the hands of lawmakers and assigning it to a less-partisan commission. Both decisions set significant precedents in the struggle for greater fairness in the American electoral system. Another consequential case (which I discuss in the epilogue) looms for October Term 2015. The justices have agreed to hear *Evenwel v. Abbott,* a case out of Texas asking whether states can draw lines based on a district's total population (as all currently do) or whether they must count only eligible voters—a formula that leaves out children, noncitizens, and felons and would work to the advantage of Republicans, since conservatives tend to live in rural areas where there are higher concentrations of eligible voters.

Alabama Legislative Black Caucus v. Alabama

In 1870, the Fifteenth Amendment to the United States Constitution formally opened the franchise to black males. It would take another amendment (the Nineteenth) and another century, however, for black men and women to enjoy a right to vote that was not severely curtailed by literacy tests, poll taxes, violence, and intimidation. The Voting Rights Act, passed in 1965, attempted to actualize the promise of the Fifteenth Amendment by combating various forms of racial discrimination at the polls. Some provisions of the law focused on seven states with particularly checkered records: Alabama, Alaska, Georgia, Louisiana, Mississippi, South Carolina, Virginia, and certain parts of North Carolina. The Voting Rights Act required these states to "preclear" any changes to their voting or election laws with the federal government lest they try to dilute black voters' power or to put stumbling blocks in the way of blacks trying to register to vote.

Over the past fifty years, the Voting Rights Act has been amended several times, and the list of states requiring preclearance has expanded. Yet Alabama remained a "covered" state until 2014, when, in *Shelby County v. Holder,* the Supreme Court knocked down the act's coverage formula as inconsistent with the Constitution's principles of federalism and commitment to state sovereignty. The act may have been reaffirmed by a vote of 98–0 in the Senate in 2006, but because it relied on "40-year-old facts having no logical relationship to the present day" to identify states that tend to engage in racial discrimination in voting practices, Chief Justice Roberts wrote, section 4(b) of the law was anachronistic and unconstitutional.

The complex facts in *Alabama Legislative Black Caucus v. Alabama* involve Alabama's problematic means of purporting to comply with the Voting Rights Act. In the wake of the 2010 census, Alabama redrew its state legislative districts to keep percentages of black voters in "majority-minority" districts (i.e., districts where blacks are a majority of voters) very close to where the proportions stood prior to 2010. This rejiggering of the boundaries was designed, Alabama claimed, to avoid reducing racial minorities' "ability to elect their preferred candidates of choice" under section 5 of the law. But black lawmakers and voters interpreted the new maps quite differently. Groups including the Alabama Legislative Black Caucus and the Alabama Democratic Conference cried foul, contending that Alabama's new districts packed black voters into electoral ghettos—not in order to enhance their ability to elect their choice of candidates but to prevent them from having influence in other state races. This, the plaintiffs charged, represented an unconstitutional "racial gerrymander," a boundary-drawing endeavor motivated by racial considerations in violation of the equal protection clause of the Fourteenth Amendment.

A lively oral argument on November 12, 2014, left it unclear how the justices would rule. When Richard Pildes, arguing against Alabama's redistricting maps, opened by saying that the state had employed "rigid racial quotas" and "rigid racial targets" in violation of the Fourteenth Amendment, Chief Justice Roberts responded that Alabama faced a dilemma in drawing its district lines. On the one hand, state officials had to ensure that there were enough minority voters in certain districts to make their favored candidates electable. But on the other hand, Alabama couldn't "pack" *too many* blacks into a district. "They have to hit this sweet spot between those two extremes without taking race predominantly into consideration?" Roberts asked. Pildes admitted that this puts states "in a bind." But he insisted, as did the United States Department of Justice, which is charged with enforcing the act, that as long as the percentages of minority voters do not fall precipitously enough to make their candidates of choice electable, no harm is done to the Voting Rights Act. Roberts would not accept this. "I think that if Alabama had reduced the number of minority voters in majority-minority districts in any significant way," he said, "the Attorney General would have come down on them like a ton of bricks."

Arguing for Alabama was Andrew Brasher, the state's solicitor general. Brasher repeated the district court's finding that "race did not predominate" in Alabama's post-2010 district-line drawing. The trick in the hearing, and the trick for any case of this type, is to decide whether a state gerrymander was undertaken in a purely partisan way (which, the court has held, usually comports with the Constitution) or whether the maps were predominantly informed by impermissible considerations of the voters' race. Only the latter, according to the 1993 case *Shaw v. Reno*, is constitutionally suspect and must be evaluated under strict scrutiny. In an exchange with Pildes, Justice Ginsburg inquired into the ontological question of how to view the maps: by looking at the state a whole or by considering the effects of the reapportionment district by district. Pildes said that since Alabama had a "common policy applied to every district in the state," a more fine-grained analysis is unnecessary.

When the justices issued their decision on March 25, 2015, a 5–4 holding with Justice Kennedy siding with the court's liberals, a granular, district-by-district analysis is precisely what they called for. Justice Breyer's majority opinion opened by stating that the federal district court that originally heard the case "applied incorrect legal standards in evaluating the claims" of the plaintiffs. The three-judge panel erred in applying a state-wide analysis rather than looking at how each district fared under the new maps. The rule against considering race in reapportionment "applies district-by-district," Justice Breyer wrote. "It does not apply to a state considered as an undifferentiated 'whole.'"

The Supreme Court also held that the district court mistakenly bought Alabama's doe-eyed claim that it was only trying to comply with the Voting Rights Act in transferring large numbers of African Americans into majority-minority districts. There is no such requirement under section 5 of the law, Justice Breyer wrote. All the law prohibits is a change that "has the purpose of or will have the effect of diminishing the ability of [the minority group] to elect their preferred candidates of choice." It does not demand "any predetermined or fixed demographic percentages" of minority voters and certainly did not require Alabama's overzealous efforts to pack black voters in such high numbers into the same districts.

In ruling for the plaintiffs, the court did not take the additional step of nullifying Alabama's 2012 reapportionment maps. Instead, it vacated the district court's judgment upholding the gerrymander and remanded it for rehearing. In other words, the case will now bounce back down to the district court, which, suitably admonished by the nation's highest court, is charged with considering district-by-district evidence, including "further evidence" it "shall reasonably find appropriate." Where this leaves the matter is a bit unclear. In shunting the matter back down the ladder, the Supreme Court majority issued a rather stern rebuke to the lower court and made it apparent that at least some of the districts in question were unconstitutionally drawn. "[T]here is strong, perhaps overwhelming evidence," Justice Breyer wrote, "that race did predominate as a factor when the legislature drew the boundaries of Senate District 26."

But Alabama has another option that would preclude or render irrelevant an upcoming ruling against its racially motivated gerrymandering. The state could avert a loss in court by tearing up its own 2012 maps and starting over. Rick Hasen, an expert in election law at the University of California at Irvine School of Law, writes that no one should "be surprised if Alabama preempts the lawsuit by drawing new districts which are less racially conscious but still constitute a partisan gerrymander." If Alabama were to draw entirely new maps, it would be free of the preclearance requirement of section 5 of the Voting Rights Act that was gutted by the *Shelby County v. Holder* decision in 2013. But it would then be subject to the constraints of the Alabama Constitution, which prohibits the splitting of counties between districts unless necessary to comply with a federal-law obligation. In the plans challenged in *Alabama*, the state had split these counties based on the view that the Voting Rights Act required doing so in order to preserve the black populations at the same levels in the districts. With entirely new maps, county splitting would no longer be legal. Alabama Legislative Black Caucus v. Alabama is a defeat for Republicans who have manipulated their constituents using racial criteria to tighten their control on the legislature. But the ruling cannot be judged in its ultimate consequences until the final maps are drawn, whether under court control or by the legislature itself.

Arizona State Legislature v. Arizona Independent Redistricting Commission

The Alabama case presents sordid questions of racial discrimination in redistricting. But when race drops out of the analysis, as it did in 2015 in a Grand Canyon State family dispute, plenty of sketchiness remains. As Justice Alito noted in the *Alabama* oral argument, "[T]he legislature could do whatever it wants if . . . it relies purely on partisanship rather than on race." Indeed, the fundamental problem with state legislative lines is that they are drawn by the party in control of the state legislature. Both parties are guilty of stacking the deck in their own favor when they are in charge. The fox, whether clad in blue or red, serves as a lethally effective guard of the henhouse.

Seeking a way out of this cycle, a coalition of activists and elected leaders in Arizona put their heads together in 2000 and drafted Proposition 106, a ballot initiative to remove the redistricting process from the legislature's portfolio. Prop 106, approved by 56 percent of Arizona voters that fall, established an Independent Redistricting Commission charged with maximizing the number of competitive districts in Arizona and striking incumbent protection from the list of permissible considerations in the line-drawing process. Similar initiatives designed to depoliticize reapportionment and give voters the right to choose their politicians—rather than the other way around—have been adopted in twenty other states in recent years, including California, which handed redistricting duties to an independent commission in 2008.

The Arizona commission had been, by most accounts, a success—at least in the first iteration of its map-drawing. But in 2012, the Republicans in control of the Arizona state legislature looked at that result and saw an opportunity slipping away. The Arizona GOP stood to gain seats in Congress if the legislature could recapture its gerrymandering powers. So the legislature brought a lawsuit contending that the US Constitution does not permit a state to outsource the redistricting process. Article I, Section 4, they said, is clear on this: "The times, places, and manner of holding elections for Senators and Representatives shall be prescribed in each state by the legislature thereof." The argument couldn't be simpler: the independent commission is not the "legislature," so it has no power to dictate the "manner of holding elections." Only the legislature is the "legislature."

This tautology was the heart of Paul Clement's argument on behalf of Arizona's legislature in the March 2, 2015, Supreme Court hearing. Clement said Arizonans' "avowed effort to redelegate [redistricting] authority to an unelected and unaccountable commission is plainly repugnant to the Constitution's vesting of that authority in the legislatures of the states." To "cut the state legislature out entirely," Clement told the justices, is a clear violation of Article I. States with similar commissions that are "purely advisory," he said, are a different story. "[N]othing in our theory suggests that they are constitutionally problematic." But to hand the quill over to independent political cartographers is to abrogate the constitutional text and the clear intentions of the framers.

Arguing for the commission was another frequent flier at the Supreme Court bar, Seth Waxman. Waxman cited eighteenth-century dictionaries to develop his claim that "legislature" means something other than the institution bearing that title. The term extends, he said, to any "lawmaking body of the state" created by the people and thus can fairly be said to include the commission established by Arizonans in Prop 106.

Justice Anthony Kennedy raised an eyebrow at this claim. "[H]istory works very much against you," he said. "[U]ntil 1913, for close to a hundred years, many states wanted to have direct election of the senators and they had all sorts of proposals," but "not one state displaced the legislature."

In her persistent questioning of Clement, Justice Elena Kagan said there are "zillions of these laws" enacted via ballot measures that may have to be scrapped if the Supreme Court sides with the Arizona legislature. Voter ID requirements in Mississippi, voting by mail in Oregon, and the use of voting machines in Arkansas "were done by referendum or by initiative with the legislative process completely cut out," she said. "So would all those be unconstitutional as well?"

No, Clement replied. Ruling against the commission does not risk overturning any and all state referenda involving elections. The trouble with Arizona's ballot initiative is not that "somebody else got into the legislature's lane and purported to do something about elections" but that it completely cut out the legislature from its Article I responsibility.

On June 29, a closely divided Supreme Court vindicated the power of the people. Writing for herself, the court's other three liberals, and Justice Kennedy, Justice Ginsburg turned to eighteenth-century dictionaries where "legislature" is defined "capaciously." The term does not just connote an institution charged with making laws, she wrote. Rather, a legislature is "the power that makes laws," whether that power refers to elected representatives in the state assembly or the people themselves. John Locke, the seventeenth-century political philosopher whose *Two Treatises of Government* helped inspire the system of divided powers established by the American founders, held that the legislative body is subject to the "people's ultimate sovereignty."

Justice Ginsburg was not starry-eyed about the virtues of independent commissions. They have not, she acknowledged, "eliminated the inevitable partisan suspicions associated with political line-drawing." But a recent study suggests, she wrote, that "they have succeeded to a great degree" in "limiting the conflict of interest implicit in legislative control over redistricting." In sum, there is nothing radical or constitutionally suspect about a ballot measure that reassigns a crucial task of democratic government from badly behaving lawmakers to a less-partisan and less-politicized commission. "The Elections Clause," she concluded, "is not reasonably read to disarm States from adopting modes of legislation that place the lead rein in the people's hands."

In an angry dissent, Chief Justice John Roberts wrote for the conservative side of the bench in charging the majority with "deliberate constitutional evasion." Justice Ginsburg saved the Arizona initiative by stringing together "disconnected observations about direct democracy, a contorted interpretation of an irrelevant statute, and naked appeals to public policy." The chief thumbed through a number of dusty dictionaries where "legislature" is defined more narrowly as "[t]he body of men in a state or kingdom, invested with power to make and repeal laws." And the meaning of the term is "unambiguous," he wrote, when considering the seventeen references to "legislature" in the text of the Constitution. None of these can "possibly be read to mean 'the people.'" Popular sovereignty may indeed be an "animating principle" of the Constitution, as the majority contended, but "the ratification of the Constitution was the ultimate act of popular sovereignty, and the people who ratified the Elections Clause did so knowing that it assigned authority to 'the Legislature' as a representative body."

Despite the majority's brief attempt to justify its stance on originalist grounds, it appears that the five justices' commitment to good government was deeper than its fealty to the intentions of the framers. The dissenters seem to have the better of the definitional argument that "legislature," as used in the constitutional text, means something specific rather than "the people" writ large. But the narrow interpretation of the term seems out of place with broader aspirational concerns about the underpinnings of American democracy. Justice Ginsburg noted that James Madison, in Federalist No. 57, wanted legislators to have "an habitual recollection of their dependence on the people." Prop 106 does that.

If the court were to permit Arizona lawmakers to begrudge their constituents the right to weigh in on redistricting, many other state electoral reforms would suddenly be cast into doubt. There are "a host of regulations," Justice Ginsburg wrote, where the people have sought to improve democratic procedures in their states. In California, voters established permanent voter registration; in Ohio, they banned ballots permitting party-line voting; in Oregon, they changed the timetable for voter registration. These initiatives and more would be "endanger[ed]," Justice Ginsburg wrote, if the court ruled against the power of Arizonans to wrest gerrymandering from their representatives' hands.

This ruling permits voters in Arizona, California, and a few other states to retain independent redistricting commissions brought into being through ballot initiative. But the fight over Arizonans' quest to unshackle their state's legislative map from politicians isn't over. Another challenge to the Sun Devil State's commission looms next fall.

The day after handing down the *Arizona State Legislature* decision, the justices agreed to hear *Harris v. Arizona Independent Redistricting Commission,* a complaint that its post-2010 maps may have been partisan and thus not drawn in accordance with the equal protection clause. Sounding something like the obverse of the *Alabama* case analyzed previously, Republican Arizona voters say that the commission drew Republicans into already over-stuffed GOP districts to give Democrats a better chance elsewhere. It again falls to the nine presidential appointees in black robes to decide the contours of electoral democracy for 320 million Americans.

Chapter 7

Gender Equality: Pregnancy Discrimination in the Workplace

Young v. United Parcel Service

In 2012, Anne-Marie Slaughter wrote an attention-grabbing article for *The Atlantic* titled "Why Women Still Can't Have It All." Slaughter's piece was a call to arms for working mothers. Women who "have managed to be both mothers and top professionals are superhuman, rich, or self-employed," she wrote. Anyone who says otherwise is "fooling" herself. In a subsequent TED talk, Slaughter, who has worked in academia and in the US State Department, said that employers should "value family just as much as work, and understand that the two reinforce each other."

The work-life tradeoff Slaughter identified is not necessarily any easier to manage for women with less lofty professional aspirations. When Peggy Young, a driver for United Parcel Service (UPS), approached her employer to request an accommodation during her pregnancy in 2006, she hoped and expected that they would come through for her. She figured that even if UPS did not value family "*just as much* as work," in Slaughter's words, it would approve her request for a temporary light-duty assignment. Young was wrong. Rather than grant her request, supported by a doctor's note, to lift no more than twenty pounds during her pregnancy, UPS forced Young to take an unpaid leave from her job and terminated her medical benefits.

In her lawsuit against UPS, Young pointed to the Pregnancy Discrimination Act (PDA), a law passed by Congress in 1978 to protect the rights of expectant mothers in the workplace. The PDA was a direct response to a Supreme Court decision two years earlier giving employers the green light to exclude pregnant women from sickness and disability benefits. In *General Electric Company v. Gilbert,* the court said that while Title VII of the Civil Rights Act of 1964 prohibited gender discrimination, it said nothing about pregnancy per se. Pregnancy is unlike other disabling conditions, then-justice William Rehnquist wrote, because it is normally "a voluntarily undertaken and desired condition." The PDA clarified that pregnancy discrimination does, in fact, count as sex discrimination under the Civil Rights Act. And it said the following: "[W]omen affected by pregnancy, childbirth, or related medical conditions shall be treated the same for all employment-related purposes . . . as other persons not so affected but similar in their ability or inability to work."

Young figured her request would be unobjectionable. After all, UPS employees who were injured on the job, who were disabled under the terms of the Americans with Disabilities Act, or who lost their driving credentials were all eligible for "light-duty" assignments. Why wouldn't the shipping company agree to make a similar accommodation for pregnant women? But Carolyn Martin, the company's occupational health manager, turned Young down, saying that since pregnancy did not fall into any of the three categories of workers eligible for alternate assignments, UPS would not switch her to a less physically onerous job. Martin "empathize[d]" with Young and "would have loved to help her" but could not. Instead, UPS sent her packing.

UPS defended its accommodation policy as "pregnancy neutral" because it neither granted nor withheld benefits to expectant mothers on the basis of their pregnancies. The light-duty policy excludes a woman carrying a fetus just as surely as it excludes an employee who hurt his or her back lifting furniture or turned an ankle playing basketball over the weekend. No "animus" toward pregnant women, UPS contended, motivated the policy.

But Young and her defenders found subtle animus at work and argued that the PDA requires employers to offer benefits to pregnant women if those benefits are available to employees "similar in their ability or inability to work." Since, as an amicus brief noted, "the vast majority of working women will become pregnant at least once during their careers" and "62 percent of women with a birth in the previous twelve months were in the labor force," the matter directly affects the lives of millions of American women.

Judge Alysson Duncan of the Fourth Circuit Court of Appeals was unconvinced. Finding no evidence of discriminatory intent on the part of UPS nor cause to read the PDA expansively, Judge Duncan merely offered Young a hesitant statement of double-negative-diluted sympathy. "While not unsympathetic to Young's circumstances," she wrote, "we are nevertheless concerned about the problematic potential of creating rights not grounded in the text and structure of Title VII as a whole." To require employers to give pregnant women every benefit available to any other worker is to treat pregnancy "more favorably than any other basis" for a work reassignment request. A win for Peggy Young would "imbue the PDA with a preferential treatment mandate that Congress neither intended nor enacted."

On December 3, 2014, when Young's appeal was heard at the Supreme Court, Justice Antonin Scalia echoed Judge Duncan's concern. Young, he said, drawing on an analogy to trade policy, was demanding "most favored nation status" for pregnant women. On the other end of the bench, Justice Ruth Bader Ginsburg countered that UPS's position relegated expectant workers to "least favored nation" status. But Scalia and Justice Breyer pressed on with several hypothetical scenarios in which the PDA, under Young's reading, seemed to give pregnant workers unreasonably cushy treatment. As the merits brief for UPS asked, if a "CEO receives company-provided transportation as an accommodation for a back injury," must the "pregnant mailroom clerk" get the same perk because she has "the same physical capacity to work"? Sam Bagenstos, Young's lawyer, had a very good day at the lectern. But his attempt to distinguish these examples from Young's complaint did not seem to satisfy the justices.

As Bagenstos started to say that an "idiosyncratic decision by an employer to provide an accommodation to a particular employee" needn't be matched for pregnant workers, Justice Breyer shot back: "Well, I don't know that it's idiosyncratic, you see, because I don't know all the workplaces, and I can imagine that employers have all kinds of different rules for different kinds of jobs." It would be both unfair and unworkable, Breyer intimated, for employers to be compelled to offer pregnant women every benefit available to employees who are similar in their ability or inability to work.

When the lawyer for UPS, Caitlin Halligan, addressed the justices, she too faced a round of persistent questions. Justices Elena Kagan and Ginsburg were most assertive. Kagan accused UPS of "creating a kind of double redundancy" in its interpretation of the PDA by ignoring the part of the law requiring that pregnant women "shall be treated the same for all employment-related purposes" as similarly situated nonpregnant workers. Ginsburg questioned Halligan's position that the "second clause adds nothing even though Congress said 'and.'" Referring to this provision, Ginsburg told Halligan, "[Y]ou don't think that the second clause does any practical work."

When the court issued its 6–3 ruling in favor of Young on March 25, 2015, Justice Breyer, writing for the majority, found a way through the thicket by adopting a "middle ground" that Justice Kagan had sketched in the oral argument. The court did not exactly hold that UPS had violated the PDA; instead, it clarified what the law demanded, suggested that Young had a promising case, and gave her another chance to prove it at the Fourth Circuit.

Writing for himself, the three female justices, and Chief Justice Roberts, Justice Breyer rejected UPS's claim that it was in compliance with the PDA because it had not singled out Young for being pregnant. To read the law that way, the majority held, was to ignore the PDA's requirement that an employer treat pregnant workers "the same for all employment-related purposes . . . as other persons not so affected but similar in their ability or inability to work." UPS had ignored "a key congressional objective in passing the Act."

But the majority did not fully buy Young's reading of the law either. Justice Breyer returned to the trope of the oral argument, calling Young's position "most favored nation" status for pregnant women. Asking employers to offer "all pregnant workers" the same accommodations they give to *any* nonpregnant worker is unreasonable. On Young's reading, Breyer wrote, the PDA might prohibit bosses from offering extra benefits to nonpregnant employees "with particularly hazardous jobs, or those whose workplace presence is particularly needed" unless they gave these benefits to expectant mothers as well. Young didn't demand a company car or free massages; she simply requested an exemption from lifting heavy parcels. But the court ruled that her interpretation of the PDA offered no way to distinguish legitimate accommodations from outlandish requests for special treatment.

After this evenhanded reprimand of both parties, Justice Breyer rolled up his sleeves and found a pragmatic solution. Applying a judicial standard developed in *McDonnell Douglas Corp v. Green,* a 1973 case involving racial discrimination, the majority explained what Young needed to do to continue to press her claim at the Fourth Circuit. She must show she is a member of a protected class (i.e., that she was pregnant), that she requested an accommodation (she did), that UPS refused to grant the accommodation (it did), and that "that the employer did accommodate others 'similar in their ability or inability to work.'" If Young shows all this and UPS cannot give a good reason why it refused to accommodate her, prospects for a win in the lower court look excellent.

In a biting dissent joined by Justices Thomas and Kennedy, Justice Antonin Scalia taunted Justice Breyer for "inventing" a new law that is "splendidly unconnected with the text and even the legislative history" of the statute in question. "Faced with two conceivable readings of the Pregnancy Discrimination Act, the court chooses neither," Scalia wrote. "It crafts instead a new law" using an interpretation that is "as dubious in principle as it is senseless in practice." He also lambasted his usual ally, Justice Alito, who concurred in the result, for "fashioning . . . a compromise" that is "text free." The PDA only prohibits targeting pregnant workers for less favorable treatment, Justice Scalia wrote. It would be illegal, for example, to buy a new ergonomic chair for a male employee who sustains a back injury on the job but to refuse to do the same for a pregnant woman with an identical injury. But pregnancy itself, Justice Scalia insisted, does not give rise to any special consideration.

Despite its characteristic vehemence, Scalia's dissent never adequately explains what role remains for the second half of the PDA under this very narrow reading. The dissenters seem not to care what Congress was trying to do when it passed the law, spurred by a rejection of *General Electric Company v. Gilbert,* in 1978. But Scalia lodged a reasonable complaint that Justice Breyer's pragmatic opinion may have "bungled the dichotomy between claims of disparate treatment and claims of disparate impact." These are, as Justice Scalia wrote, two distinct ways to prove discrimination under Title VII of the Civil Rights Act. "Disparate treatment," or intentional discrimination, can be difficult to prove, as it involves an investigation of motives. "Disparate impact," on the other hand (which I discuss at length in chapter 5), involves "using a practice that 'fall[s] more harshly on one group than another and cannot be justified by business necessity.'" Scalia wrote that the "topsy-turvy world created by today's decision" allows a pregnant woman to "establish disparate treatment by showing that the effects of her employer's policy fall more harshly on pregnant women than on others," mixing up two ideas with "different standards of liability, different defenses, and different remedies."

This may be a feature of the ruling even Justice Breyer seems to recognize as troublesome. During the oral argument in December, Justice Breyer had complained to Sam Bagenstos, Young's lawyer, that under a disparate-impact claim, the analysis would be more straightforward. It would have been "a quite easy way for you to win," he said. With a sigh, Breyer lamented, "but you didn't bring the disparate [impact] claim and, therefore, what am I to do?" The alternative, Breyer said then, would be to "twist" the disparate treatment claim "out of shape."

Recasting the PDA with a *McDonnell Douglas* face, Justice Scalia charged, is indeed to "twist" Title VII jurisprudence "out of shape." The approach imports an analytical edifice that may make it difficult for employers to understand exactly what the PDA requires them to do. A report from labor and employment law firm Ogletree Deakins advised that "*Young* . . . requires prudent employers to evaluate their current policies and practices to determine whether they significantly burden pregnant workers and, if they do, whether the non-discriminatory reasons for the policies or practices justify that burden." Those reasons cannot be simply that it's cheaper or more convenient to treat pregnant women differently from other employees who are similar in their capacity to do their jobs.

Faced with two unsavory readings of the PDA, Justice Breyer found a plausible middle ground that, Bagenstos told me, "get us nearly all of what we wanted." The decision "basically takes [Young's] analysis and packag[es] it into *McDonnell Douglas*," he said. The disparate-impact claim may have appealed to Justice Breyer, but the rest of the bench is another story. The claim probably "wouldn't even have made it to the court," Bagenstos said, "and would certainly have had less than five votes."

Recent developments temper the drama of the ruling in *Young*. In a curious move, UPS announced just before the oral arguments that as of January 1, 2015, it will provide light-duty assignments to pregnant employees who request them. And nine states, prior to the *Young* ruling, passed laws requiring similar short-term accommodations. But with *Young*, clunky as it is, the Pregnancy Discrimination Act now has a clearer message to employers: it isn't enough to simply resist punishing employees for their pregnancies. If an expectant mother in your employ needs an accommodation and you provide a similar accommodation to other similarly situated employees, you can't withhold it from the pregnant worker. That message is a welcome one for millions of working American women of child-bearing age.

Chapter 8

The Separation of Powers: Congress, the President, and Foreign Policy

Zivotofsky v. Kerry

What would spark a Supreme Court case pitting a twelve-year-old boy named Menachem Zivotofsky against John Kerry, the Secretary of State? One of the most contentious flashpoints of international diplomacy in the past fifty years: the Israeli-Palestinian dispute.

At issue is a single line in Menachem's US passport. The boy was born to American parents in 2002 in a hospital in Jerusalem, and when he received his first passport, "Jerusalem" was listed as his place of birth. Passports typically list both the city and country of birth when American citizens are born outside the United States: "Seoul, South Korea," for example, or "Berlin, Germany." So why just "Jerusalem" rather than "Jerusalem, Israel"?

In the decades since the State of Israel achieved independence in 1948, the American government has maintained a policy of neutrality with regard to sovereignty over Jerusalem. The city is home to holy sites for Muslims, Christians, and Jews, and has been governed by all three religious groups during various periods over the millennia. In the past five centuries, Jerusalem has been handed from the Ottomans to the British and then to the joint rule of Israel (in the west) and Jordan (in the east). In the wake of the Six Day War of 1967, when Israel was attacked by Arab armies on three fronts, Israel annexed East Jerusalem, including the walled Old City, and in 1980 formally declared Jerusalem its "complete and united" capital in its quasi-constitutional basic legislation.

As the Palestinian movement grew in the 1980s and 1990s, it became increasingly strident in opposition to Israel's continued control over the city it calls Al Quds, or "the city of peace." Negotiations between Israel and the Palestinians over the status of Jerusalem are at a decades-old impasse, with each side insisting on conditions the other categorically rejects. Having gained control of the Jews' holiest site, the Western Wall, for the first time in two thousand years, and having established a Jewish presence throughout the city, Israel refuses to redivide it. But the Palestinians insist that East Jerusalem will be the capital of any future Palestinian state.

The United States has facilitated peace negotiations between the contending parties since the 1970s. In order to maintain itself as an honest broker in the peace process, the American government has been at pains to avoid recognizing Israel as the exclusive sovereign over Jerusalem. The final status of the holy city, the policy holds, should be determined through negotiations between Israelis and Palestinians. It is not for the United States to prejudge the question.

Which brings us back to Menachem Zivotofsky and a law passed just months before he was born. In section 214(d) of the Foreign Relations Authorization Act,

Congress provided that for the "purposes of the registration of birth, certification of nationality, or issuance of a passport of a United States citizen born in the city of Jerusalem, the Secretary shall, upon the request of the citizen or the citizen's legal guardian, record the place of birth as Israel." President George W. Bush signed the massive bill but issued a signing statement clarifying that he would not enforce section 214(d). "[I]f construed as mandatory rather than advisory," he wrote, it "impermissibly interfere[s] with the President's constitutional authority to formulate the position of the United States, speak for the Nation in international affairs, and determine the terms on which recognition is given to foreign states." So when Menachem's mother made a request to add "Israel" to her son's passport, the State Department refused.

Suing in a federal district court, the Zivotofskys' claim was initially thrown out for lack of standing and because the family's complaint implicated a "political question" that courts normally avoid addressing. The District of Columbia Court of Appeals ruled there was standing but agreed it was a nonjusticiable political question. Having lost twice, the family petitioned the Supreme Court and got a hearing in *Zivotofsky v. Clinton*. In 2012, the Supreme Court ruled 8–1 in their favor, rejecting the political question defense. "[T]he Judiciary must decide if Zivotofsky's interpretation of the statute is correct, and whether the statute is constitutional," the justices held. This is a legal question, Chief Justice John Roberts wrote for the majority, and it is quite distinct from the court deigning to weigh in on whether Jerusalem is or is not part of Israel. The justices are not charged with making foreign policy, but they are responsible for clarifying what ought to happen when two coordinate branches of government grab the same cookie and refuse to share.

Kicked back to the DC appeals court, the case's name changed to *Zivotofsky v. Kerry* because John Kerry had replaced Hillary Clinton as Secretary of State. This time, with instructions from the Supreme Court to go ahead and rule on the merits of the claim, the DC court agreed with the president. Congress overstepped its bounds when writing section 214(d), the judges held: "The President exclusively holds the power to determine whether to recognize a foreign sovereign."

When the Supreme Court agreed to hear the case a second time—this time on the substance of the matter rather than on technicalities—the issue was already familiar to the justices. At the oral argument on November 3, 2014, Alyza Lewin, the Zivotofskys' lawyer, opened by denying that Congress was interfering in the least with the president's power to recognize foreign governments. Permitting a Jerusalem-born American to list Israel as his place of birth "gives the individuals a choice and does not confer formal recognition," she said. That is "certainly a reasonable position," Justice Breyer responded, but the administration disagrees. The solicitor general says that section 214(d) "unconstitutionally encroaches on the President's core recognition authority." So it's a question of *he said, she said*. "How can I say that I'm right even if I agree with you," Justice Breyer asked, "and they, who are in charge of foreign affairs, are wrong when they make those two statements, which certainly sound plausible"?

Justice Kagan worried that section 214(d) was "a very selective vanity plate law," since it did not give American citizens born in Jerusalem the right to have "Palestine" printed on their passports. "That suggests," she observed, "that Congress had a view, and the view was that Jerusalem was properly part of Israel." If so, it seems hard to maintain that acting on the law would have no implications for American recognition of Israel as the legitimate sovereign over Jerusalem.

When Donald Verrilli, the solicitor general, took the lectern, he said that "the fundamental problem with Section 214(d)" is that it "forc[es] the Executive Branch to issue official diplomatic communications that contradict the position of the United States." Besides, he said later, "recognition is not lawmaking. It is an executive function." Facing pushback mainly from Chief Justice Roberts and Justices Scalia and Alito, Solicitor General Verrilli stuck to his guns.

Most of the discussion focused on how to know when a government is recognizing a foreign power. Is it when the Secretary of State agrees to list "Israel" on a passport? Or when Congress passes a law instructing the Secretary of State to do so? Or when a president signs such a law (despite the caveats implied in a signing statement)? The discussion smacked of debates in literary theory over whether the meaning of a text is found in the intentions of the author, in the reader's interpretation, or somewhere in between.

Only in Lewin's final four minutes of rebuttal did the discussion turn squarely to the question of America's constitutional structure and whether the executive or legislative branch of the federal government has the power to recognize foreign nations. Without time for much back-and-forth, Lewin argued that "[a]llowing the State

Department's say-so to control because it's an expert in foreign relations would be abdicating an independent function." It would, she said, "turn the President into an autocrat."

Reading Justice Kennedy's 6–3 decision against her clients seven months later in the June 8, 2015, decision, Lewin may have lamented not spending more time on this final point. Justice Kennedy quickly dismissed the proposition that 214(d) had nothing to do with recognition of Israel. What the Secretary of State records in official documents does imply something about the position of the federal government. By granting citizens' requests to list their birthplace as Israel when they are born in Jerusalem, members of Congress contravene the president's policy. Congress "cannot require [the president] to contradict his own statement regarding a determination of formal recognition," he wrote.

Justice Kennedy spent the bulk of the twenty-nine pages of his opinion diving deep into the history of US presidents and foreign recognition. He first examined the so-called reception clause in Article II, Section 3 of the Constitution. When the founders wrote that the president "shall receive Ambassadors and other public Ministers," they strongly hinted that he gets to choose which ambassadors and public ministers to receive. When a president receives a foreign leader, that is "tantamount to recognizing the sovereignty of the sending state," Justice Kennedy wrote, quoting Alexander Hamilton and using the example of President George Washington, who "acknowledged the republic of France, by the reception of its minister."

The president's recognition prerogative is "further supported by his additional Article II powers," the majority opinion continued, specifically the power to make treaties. "Beyond that, the President himself has the power to open diplomatic channels simply by engaging in direct diplomacy with foreign heads of state and their ministers. The Constitution thus assigns the President means to effect recognition on his own initiative. Congress, by contrast, has no constitutional power that would enable it to initiate diplomatic relations with a foreign nation." In sum, "it is for the President alone to make the specific decision of what foreign power he will recognize as legitimate."

The three dissenting justices in *Zivotofsky* did not buy this analysis. In a terse, irritable dissent, Chief Justice Roberts called the court's decision "unprecedented" and "a first." The Court has "never before" permitted "a president's direct defiance of an Act of Congress in the field of foreign affairs," he wrote. The reception clause appears in a section of Article II outlining the "*duties*" of a president, not his powers, and the court's prior rulings imply no such "sweeping understanding of executive power." Presidents Andrew Jackson and Abraham Lincoln were "not generally known for their cramped conceptions of presidential power," Chief Justice Roberts quipped. But even these muscular chief executives "expressed uncertainty" about whether they enjoyed an exclusive power to recognize other states. Echoing the Zivotofskys' main contention in the oral argument, Chief Justice Roberts used italics in making his next point. Even if "the President does have exclusive recognition power, he still cannot prevail in this case, because the statute at issue *does not implicate recognition.*"

The longer, more searching dissenting opinion was written by Justice Scalia, and both Justice Alito and the chief signed on to it. In an interesting and rare two-pronged attack, Justice Scalia took on both Justice Kennedy and his usual ally, Justice Thomas, with equal vehemence. The founders, Justice Scalia wrote, did not give presidents an exclusive power in foreign affairs. "The People of the United States had other ideas when they organized our Government." They envisioned "a sound structure of balanced powers" that is "essential to the preservation of just government." The government's relations with other nations "formed no exception to that principle."

In his concurring opinion, Justice Thomas held for the administration on the grounds that Congress had no specific constitutional authority to pass section 214(d). Drawing on Chief Justice John Marshall's famous line from *McCulloch v. Maryland* that "it is a *constitution* we are expounding," Justice Scalia argued that Congress was well within its powers to weigh in on passport rules. He also dipped into his well of irascible one-liners. Justice Thomas's expansive interpretation of presidential power "turns the Constitution upside-down," he wrote. It "shatters . . . congressional power over foreign affairs . . . in one stroke" and countenances "a presidency more reminiscent of George III than George Washington."

A one-paragraph concurring opinion from Justice Breyer reiterated his position from the initial hearing of *Zivotofsky* in 2012 that the case poses a political question the Supreme Court would have been wise to take a pass on in the first place. But since the court ruled otherwise in 2012, Justice Breyer reluctantly joined the majority. The pragmatist justice's worries were, predictably, legitimized when the decision was handed down. Mahmoud Abbas, the Palestinian president, called *Zivotofsky* "an important decision which accords with international resolutions," while Jerusalem's mayor criticized the court's ruling, saying the city "is and always will be the capital of Israel."

Aside from these initial reactions, the fallout from the decision on Israeli-Palestinian negotiations seems temporary and minor. There are plenty of obstacles to Middle East peacemaking more troublesome than the details of what is or isn't etched into American passports. And it is unlikely that very many Jerusalem-born American Jews will be devastated by the Supreme Court's decision preventing them from listing "Israel" on their passports.

But *Zivotofsky* could have wider implications, as George Washington University law professor Alan Morrison has suggested. "President Obama may well decide to fight Congress on matters such as an arms agreement with Iran and his authority to negotiate trade agreements, even without exercising his constitutional veto," Morrison writes. "Or he might announce that he has recognized the Castro-led Cuban government, with no worry about an effort of Congress to override him." But *Zivotofsky* does not hand exclusive foreign-policy powers to the executive. "Although the president alone effects the formal act of recognition," Justice Kennedy wrote in the majority opinion, "Congress' powers, and its central role in making laws, give it substantial authority regarding many of the policy determinations that precede and follow the act of recognition itself." This means presidents cannot accomplish much without the cooperation of lawmakers. "Formal recognition may seem a hollow act," the majority noted, "if it is not accompanied" by moves only Congress can make: "the dispatch of an ambassador, the easing of trade restrictions, and the conclusion of treaties." With *Zivotofsky* on the books, presidents get to say which parts of which countries earn American recognition. But Congress still has leverage in shaping the nature of international relationships.

Chapter 9

The Fate of Obamacare:
The ACA Survives, Again

King v. Burwell

The Patient Protection and Affordable Care Act (ACA), the national health overhaul more popularly known as Obamacare, became law in 2010. Since then, Republicans in Congress have rarely paused in their crusade against Barack Obama's signature legislative achievement. The House of Representatives has staged votes to repeal the law more than fifty times and managed enough yeas to do that on four occasions. The Senate, held by Democrats until January 2015, has thus far not reciprocated. If and when the now-Republican upper chamber joins the House to repeal the ACA, President Obama will be waiting with his veto pen.

While these symbolic expressions of distaste for Obamacare have been steadily emanating from the Capitol, the real drama has been across First Street, Northeast, at the institution Google Maps calls the nation's "monumental decision-making institution." In *National Federation of Independent Business (NFIB) v. Sebelius,* in 2012, the Supreme Court narrowly upheld the constitutionality of the law's "individual mandate," the requirement that most Americans buy themselves health insurance policies. In 2014, the court ruled that the religious scruples of some business owners earned them an exemption from the so-called contraceptive mandate, the ACA's requirement that businesses provide female employees with birth control devices and medications. For all its significance as an expansion of religious freedom, the latter case, *Burwell v. Hobby Lobby,* did not represent a challenge striking at the heart of Obamacare; it carved out a narrow exemption for one type of corporation from one of the ACA's many stipulations.

So a year later, when the justices once again opted to weigh in on the most contentious policy question of Barack Obama's presidency, Obamacare's supporters feared the worst. After surprising almost everyone in the 2012 case by voting with the court's liberal justices to save the act, some observers thought Chief Justice John Roberts was poised to even the score and deliver a win for conservatives. When the justices agreed to hear the case in November of 2014, venerable *New York Times* Supreme Court reporter Linda Greenhouse declared the development more worrisome than the decision in *Bush v. Gore*, the 2000 decision that handed George W. Bush the keys to the White House. Granting certiorari in *King v. Burwell* was, Greenhouse wrote, "a naked power grab by conservative justices."

But this time, in contrast to *NFIB v. Sebelius,* the dispute had nothing to do with the United States Constitution. The question in *King v. Burwell* was literally semantic. At issue was whether the Treasury Department interpreted four words of the phone-book-sized statute ("established by the State") correctly when developing its rule for allocating tax credits to Americans buying health insurance policies under the law.

To understand this case, we first need to recall how the ACA sought to expand health care coverage for Americans. It is a strategy in three parts. First, the law addressed a long-standing conundrum facing sick, uninsured Americans whose "preexisting conditions" either disqualified them from coverage or made coverage prohibitively expensive. The ACA told insurers they could no longer deny coverage or jack up premiums based on a subscriber's medical history; they must welcome all comers. Second, to compensate insurance companies for the bigger claims they would pay out for customers with, say, cancer or diabetes, the law expanded the pool of insured Americans by insisting, with certain exceptions, that everybody—including the young and the healthy—buy a policy. (This was the "individual mandate" that survived a constitutional challenge in 2012.) Third, to make these policies affordable for poor and moderate-income Americans, the law provided tax subsidies to individuals earning up to four times the federal poverty level. This means that a family of four with an annual income of $95,000 or less would qualify for federal help to secure health insurance. To facilitate these purchases, the law asked states to establish virtual marketplaces (or, in the lingo of the law, "exchanges") that would be "one-stop shopping" sites for a range of health insurance policies. Bowing to principles of federalism, though, the law could not *require* states to set up these exchanges, so the ACA included a backup plan: the Department of Health and Human Services would set up federally run exchanges in states that declined to do so themselves.

It sometimes takes a nosy libertarian or two to rain on a parade, and that's just what happened in 2011, when Jonathan Adler, a law professor at the Case Western Reserve University School of Law, jumped on a quirk in the text of the ACA spotted the previous fall by eagle-eyed Tom Christina, a New York attorney for the law firm Ogletree Deakins. The textual peculiarity would bring the law under Supreme Court review four years later. In 2013, Adler and Michael Cannon, a Cato Institute scholar, coauthored a law review article, "Taxation without Representation: The Illegal IRS Rule to Expand Tax Credits under the PPACA." Adler and Cannon pointed out that the ACA's language regarding subsidies for low- and moderate-income Americans is specific to marketplaces that are "established by the State."

When the Internal Revenue Service developed rules for dispensing the subsidies, Adler and Cannon charge, it ignored this language and provided the benefits to Americans buying their insurance policies via exchanges established by the federal government as well as by the states. Since only sixteen states had opted to set up their own exchanges, upward of eight million Americans in thirty-four states were receiving tax subsidies that the law did not countenance.

The feat accomplished by Adler and Cannon should not be understated: they found what they hoped was a four-word poison pill tucked into a mammoth haystack of words in the nearly one-thousand-page piece of legislation. The revelation soon served as the genesis for several lawsuits against the IRS subsidy allocations. On July 22, 2014, contradictory decisions came from two federal appellate courts: the Fourth Circuit and the Circuit for the District of Columbia. By a 2-1 margin, a three-judge panel of the DC Circuit found for the law's challengers. The court concluded (in *Halbig v. Burwell*) that "the ACA unambiguously restricts the . . . subsidy to insurance purchased on Exchanges 'established by the State.'"

Just a few hours later that same day, the Fourth Circuit evened the score when it delivered a win for the ACA in *King v. Burwell*. While a concurring judge fully adopted the government's position that the law's structure and purpose require the provision of subsidies to everyone, regardless of whether they bought health insurance through state or federal exchanges, the majority were more circumspect. The court said it "cannot ignore the common-sense appeal of the plaintiffs' argument." The government's position is, it said, "only slightly" stronger than the challengers' argument. But in the end, under a doctrine known as the *Chevron* deference, the Fourth Circuit judges found for the government. (The *Chevron* doctrine holds that when a law is ambiguous enough to admit of multiple interpretations, a federal agency's reading of the law must only be "reasonable," not necessarily the best or the only reading.) The "statutory language is ambiguous and subject to multiple interpretations," the ruling read, so "the rule [is] a permissible exercise of the agency's discretion."

Ordinarily, the Supreme Court will agree to hear a high-profile case when there is a split in the circuit courts. But the split between the Fourth Circuit and the DC Circuit with regard to the ACA was effectively put on hold in September when the latter court announced it would rehear the *Halbig* case before the entire slate of seventeen judges. It looked as if the justices had jumped the gun, then, when they announced they would hear *King v. Burwell* two months later, before the DC Circuit had reconsidered *Halbig*. An *en banc* decision for the government would have aligned the DC Circuit with the Fourth Circuit, wiping away the circuit-court split and making Supreme Court review much less likely. So it was curious timing on the part of the justices. Were the court's conservatives eager to grant the case before the circuit split was eliminated to give them another shot at upending a health care law they despised? Or were the liberal justices confident they could give Obamacare another lease on life?

We do not know which justices voted to hear *King v. Burwell*. All we know is that at least four of them did so. In the four months between the cert grant and the oral argument, all anyone could do was speculate on where the debate would focus or which points would be most persuasive to Chief Justice John Roberts and Justice Anthony Kennedy, the only two justices widely expected to be in play. Only one would need to join the court's liberals to save Obamacare.

In the pleadings stage leading up to the early March oral argument, there was, of course, the textual matter of how to make sense of those fateful words: "established by the State." That was the heart of the plaintiffs' challenge. But there were four more questions beyond the narrow interpretive matter that emerged:

1. Do the plaintiffs really have the legal right, the status known as "standing," to bring the case? In order to present a "case or controversy" before a court, a plaintiff must suffer a tangible harm. In

the early months of 2015, several reports emerged that the four Virginians named in the *King* suit may not have been subject to the ACA penalty for failing to carry an insurance policy and therefore may have been ineligible to sue.

2. Will the Supreme Court follow the Fourth Circuit in deciding the case on grounds of the *Chevron* deference?

3. Will the widely reported expectation that eight million Americans will lose their health insurance, should the plaintiffs win, affect the justices' decision making? What about the anticipated "death spiral" that would raise insurance rates dramatically for the smaller remaining subscriber pool, forcing more Americans to drop their insurance and undermining the law's mission of lowering prices and expanding access to health care?

4. Does it violate bedrock principles of federalism to coerce the states into establishing their own health care exchanges? This query, posed by Yale law professor Abbe Gluck late in the pre–oral argument commentary, asked whether the relationship between the federal government and the states would be infringed if the plaintiffs' interpretation of the law should prevail. Giving states a "choice" between setting up an exchange and giving up billions of dollars in tax subsidies for their citizens, Gluck pointed out, has the flavor of federal extortion. And in a key amicus brief, twenty-three states claimed they had no prior notice that federal subsidies were conditional on having a state-established exchange.

The oral argument on March 4 concerning the latest—and probably last—battle in what Justice Elena Kagan called a "never-ending saga" of Obamacare challenges did not disappoint. In a rematch of their 2012 showdown, Solicitor General Donald Verrilli and brash Washington lawyer Michael Carvin went toe-to-toe for eighty minutes, fielding tough questions from an impeccably prepared bench of justices. Each of the four matters noted previously came up in some form during the hearing. The question of standing, however, saw only a brief period of intense questioning during the first few minutes of each lawyer's argument and seemed to end with a whimper. Verrilli essentially granted the argument to the petitioner.

Carvin opened by calling *King* "a straightforward case of statutory construction where the plain language of the statute dictates the result." Justice Breyer shook his head. "What's the problem," he asked, with viewing a federal exchange as the functional equivalent of state-run markets? After Breyer and Carvin traded some technical mumbo-jumbo, Justice Kagan blessedly stepped in to pose one of her trademark hypotheticals: "So I have three clerks, Mr. Carvin. Their names are Will and Elizabeth and Amanda. Okay? So . . . I say, Will, I'd like you to write me a memo. And I say, Elizabeth, I want you to edit Will's memo once he's done. And then I say, Amanda, listen, if Will is too busy to write the memo, I want you to write such memo. Now, my question is: If Will is too busy to write the memo and Amanda has to write such memo, should Elizabeth edit the memo?"

The question matches up nicely to *King v. Burwell*. To be perhaps too clear about the analogy, think of Will as one of the fifty states. The ACA asks the state to set up an exchange but provides for a backup solution should the state, for one reason or another, fail to do so. That fallback is the federal government—Amanda in the hypothetical— which sets up the exchange in the state's stead. Now that Amanda is writing the memo, since Will is unavailable, and given that Elizabeth was tasked with editing Will's memo, what is Elizabeth to do? She was never explicitly told to edit a memo that *Amanda* wrote. So does she take an early lunch? Of course not. And not just because clerks for Supreme Court justices are ill advised to have lunch anywhere but at their desks. Elizabeth goes ahead and edits Amanda's memo, since Amanda was filling in for Will when she drafted it. That's because Elizabeth's job is *to edit the memo,* no matter who writes it. (The memo needs to be edited, no matter its author.) Likewise, the insurance subsidies are designed *to make it easier for poor and moderate-income Americans to buy health insurance,* no matter whether the state or the federal government set up the exchange. (Low-income Americans need subsidies to buy health care, no matter which state they call home.) The Department of Health and Human Services would be cutting off the law's nose to spite its face if it instructed the IRS to give tax subsidies only to people buying insurance on the state exchanges.

Verrilli amplified the implications of Justice Kagan's question during his turn before the dais. The plaintiffs' challenge "makes a mockery" of the ACA and leads to a "textual brick wall," he said, "revok[ing] the promise of affordable care" at the heart of the law. In response, Justice Scalia grumbled that while "it may not be the statute they intended," it is "the statute that they wrote." Only

Congress, not the justices, he said, has the authority to "rewrite" a bad law.

Going into the oral argument, everyone was fairly sure how seven of the nine justices would vote. Justices Alito, Scalia, and Thomas seemed like sure bets to pounce on Obamacare's technical difficulty to once again register a vote of no confidence in the law, while Justices Breyer, Ginsburg, Kagan, and Sotomayor would view the challenge as frivolous. All eyes, then, were on Chief Justice Roberts, who defected to the liberal side in 2012, and Justice Kennedy, the perennial swing vote.

Roberts kept everyone guessing. He was all but silent throughout the hearing and, when he did open his mouth, refused to join his colleagues in pointed questioning. Justice Kennedy, on the other hand, perked everyone's ears in the courtroom when he said to Carvin that coercing states to set up their own exchanges raised a "serious constitutional question" of federalism. He essentially gave voice to Abbe Gluck's concern that the federal government oversteps its bounds when it forces states to establish an exchange lest they deprive their residents of millions of dollars in tax breaks.

On June 8, two-and-a-half weeks before the decision in *King v. Burwell* arrived, President Barack Obama breached presidential protocol in weighing in on a pending Supreme Court case. At a press conference, Obama criticized the justices for deigning to hear *King*. Only a "twisted interpretation of four words in . . . a couple-thousand-page piece of legislation" would allow the court to eliminate tax subsidies for health insurance in thirty-four states. *King* "should be an easy case," he said. "Frankly, it probably shouldn't even have been taken up." These comments no doubt piqued some of the conservative justices, but on June 25, the day before the court released its decision making same-sex marriage a constitutional right, Obama got his wish. The justices voted 6–3 to uphold the federal subsidies and save the Affordable Care Act from a near-certain death. Neither the administration nor Republicans in Congress had a plausible plan B ready in case the decision would have come out the other way.

Chief Justice John Roberts—joined this time by Justice Kennedy—once again left his most conservative colleagues behind and refused to tamper with the Affordable Care Act. Writing for six justices, Roberts turned back the semantic objection in a crisp, lawyerly twenty-one-page opinion. And for the second time in three years, he was booed by conservative commentators. In a widely expressed sentiment, Curt Levey of the Committee for Justice said that "John Roberts, a Bush appointee, is now dead to conservatives." Michael Cannon of the Cato Institute was a bit more tempered. *King* "validated President Obama's massive power grab," he said, and shows that the Supreme Court has "allowed itself to be intimidated."

But the most remarkable aspect of Chief Justice Roberts's majority opinion is a few pages in which he presents a cheerfully lucid account of the crisis in the American health care system and how the Affordable Care Act attempts to address it. The summary is pithier and clearer than anything the Obama administration ever put out; it almost has the ring of a brochure for Obamacare. The three features of the law (universal coverage, the individual mandate, and the subsidies), Roberts wrote, are "interlocking" and "closely intertwined." To require health insurance companies to insure everybody, even people with preexisting conditions that require costly treatments, and to require that most people buy a policy "would not work without the tax credits."

Roberts did lament that the ACA was plagued by "inartful drafting." He even said the challengers' view gives "'established by the State' . . . its most natural meaning." Yet Roberts ruled that context is key to understanding those words. It's deeply problematic, he wrote, to posit that Congress meant to severely undercut the effectiveness of its own law. "[T]here would be no 'qualified individuals' on federal exchanges" to receive subsidies, he wrote, if the law did not countenance such subsidies in the first place.

Were those subsidies to disappear, Roberts continued, adopting the rhetoric of the ACA's defenders, "the combination of no tax credits and an ineffective coverage requirement could well push a state's individual insurance market into a *death spiral*" (emphasis added), whereby premiums rise and enrollments fall. He cited research according to which premiums would increase nearly 50 percent and enrollments would plummet 70 percent. "Congress passed the Affordable Care Act to improve health insurance markets, not to destroy them," Roberts concluded. The tax credits "are necessary for the federal exchanges to function like their state exchange counterparts, and to avoid the type of calamitous result that Congress plainly meant to avoid."

Justice Scalia penned a fiery dissent, joined by Justices Alito and Thomas. It was exceeded in rhetorical flourish only by Scalia's apoplectic dissent in the same-sex marriage case, described in chapter 10. The six justices in the majority proffered an understanding of the ACA that "is of course quite absurd," Justice Scalia began. "Words no longer have meaning if an exchange that is not established by a state is 'established by the State.'" Only someone "with no semblance of shame" could contend otherwise.

What about context, the claim that the ACA should be interpreted in light of its expressed purpose to provide affordable care for all Americans? "Context always matters," Justice Scalia wrote. "I wholeheartedly agree with the court that sound interpretation requires paying attention to the whole law, not homing in on isolated words or even isolated sections." But context "is a tool for understanding the terms of the law, not an excuse for rewriting them."

This is a theme Justice Scalia has sounded consistently for almost thirty years. "Congress can enact foolish statutes as well as wise ones," he wrote in his 1997 book *A Matter of Interpretation: Federal Courts and the Law,* "and it is not for the courts to decide which is which and rewrite the former." In *King,* Scalia wrote that "context only underscores the outlandishness of the court's interpretation." The chief justice has composed a "defense of the indefensible" that "suffers from no shortage of flaws." If Congress has written a self-imploding law, so be it. The Supreme Court is not suited to rewrite bad statutes. It "has no free-floating power 'to rescue Congress from its drafting errors.'" The majority, in Justice Scalia's eyes, abrogated its judicial role in *King v. Burwell.* It is a "discouraging truth that the Supreme Court of the United States favors some laws over others, and is prepared to do whatever it takes to uphold and assist its favorites."

In the weeks leading up to the decision in *King,* President Obama declared that the Affordable Care Act "is now part of the fabric of how we care for one another. This is health care in America." Chief Justice Roberts essentially said the same thing in his ringing defense of the law in the majority opinion. Had the plaintiffs persuaded a majority of the justices of the strength of their textual quibble, subsidies to low- and moderate-income Americans would have been pulled out from under subscribers on thirty-four state exchanges, leaving many unable to afford coverage. Close to eight million Americans—roughly the population of New York City—would have lost their insurance and the broader health care market would have been thrown into turmoil.

In the end, *King v. Burwell* came down to six justices' commonsense understanding of what Congress was trying to do when it passed the Affordable Care Act—making health care more widely available and more affordable—and their unwillingness to throw millions of Americans in thirty-four states under the bus. "A fair reading of legislation," Chief Justice Roberts wrote, "demands a fair understanding of the legislative plan."

Same-Sex Marriage: "Equal Dignity" and the Constitution

Obergefell v. Hodges

The crooked path to this year's historic same-sex marriage ruling at the Supreme Court began nearly a half-century ago. In 1970, Richard Baker and James Michael McConnell, sweethearts at the University of Minnesota, requested a marriage license from a court clerk in Minneapolis. When the men were rebuffed, they sued, claiming that Minnesota's heterosexuals-only marriage law violated the Ninth and Fourteenth Amendments to the US Constitution. The Minnesota Supreme Court turned to *Webster's Third New International Dictionary* and found that "marriage" means "the state of being united to a person of the opposite sex as husband or wife." It rejected Baker and McConnell's plea, noting that traditional marriage "is as old as the book of *Genesis*." When the case *Baker v. Nelson* then reached the US Supreme Court, the justices issued a terse ruling upholding the Minnesota court's decision on the grounds that the case raises no "substantial federal question." Over the next few years, similar challenges in Kentucky (*Jones v. Hallahan*) and Washington State (*Singer v. Hara*) fizzled as well.

It took two decades for the next major challenge to state bans on same-sex marriage to appear, this time in Hawaii. In *Baehr v. Miike,* three gay couples in the Aloha State waged a meandering, nine-year legal battle to procure marriage licenses. They lost in the trial court, but on appeal, the Supreme Court of Hawaii ruled that denying marriage rights to gays amounted to sex discrimination under the Hawaiian Constitution's equal protection clause. That court sent the matter back to the lower court with instructions to reconsider the case using "strict scrutiny," a very demanding analysis that requires the state to show it has compelling reasons for treating gay couples differently from straight ones. Judge Kevin Chang's subsequent ruling in 1996 represented the first judicial win for marriage equality. Hawaii had shown no compelling reason to discriminate against the gay couples, he concluded, and must begin issuing marriage licenses to opposite-sex and same-sex couples alike.

This initial victory for gay rights, however, was pyrrhic and resulted in no marriages. While on appeal, the ruling was undercut almost immediately by an amendment to the Hawaiian Constitution approved in 1998 by ballot initiative. In light of the amendment, which gave the state the power "to reserve marriage to opposite-sex couples," Hawaii's Supreme Court ruled that the couples' appeal was now a dead letter.

Five years later, and five thousand miles to the east, the Massachusetts Supreme Judicial Court issued a marriage equality ruling that *would* stick. On May 17, 2004, the Bay State became America's first to issue marriage licenses to gays and lesbians. The backlash to this news across the country was quick and fierce. Conservative activists in eleven states ushered initiatives banning same-sex marriage onto electoral ballots, and in every one of those eleven states (Arkansas, Georgia, Kentucky, Michigan, Mississippi, Montana, North Dakota, Ohio, Oklahoma, Oregon, and Utah), the bans passed by a collective margin of 2–1.

The gay-rights movement took this sweeping denunciation of same-sex marriage as a terrible blow, but activist Roey Thorpe noted at the time that "on the road to equality and freedom, there are always setbacks." This long-view optimism, it turns out, was warranted. Looking back eleven years, it is almost unimaginable how far and how fast the case for gay marriage swept across the land.

After Massachusetts took the first step, state judicial rulings brought gay marriage to California (2008; and though this decision was later nullified by Proposition 8, litigation ultimately flipped California back toward marriage equality), Connecticut (2008), Iowa (2009), New Jersey (2013), and New Mexico (2013). Legislative acts or ballot initiatives did the same in Vermont (2009), New Hampshire (2010), New York (2011), Maine (2012), Washington (2012), Maryland (2013), Rhode Island (2013), Delaware (2013), Minnesota (2013), Hawaii (2013), and Illinois (2014). That adds up to sixteen states, plus the District of Columbia, where gays and lesbians could wed by mid-2014. But over the next few months, a cascade of federal court rulings would more than double that number. The immediate springboard to OT 2014's *Obergefell v. Hodges*, as the four challenges to state bans on gay marriage will go down in history, was the court's *United States v. Windsor* ruling in 2013. It was *Windsor* that provided dozens of federal district courts and four federal circuit courts with the reasoning to strike down gay marriage bans in the states within their jurisdictions.

In *Windsor*, the court nullified a central provision of the Defense of Marriage Act (DOMA), a law that sailed through Congress and garnered President Bill Clinton's signature in 1996. DOMA addressed conservative anxiety over the prospect that states would begin legalizing same-sex marriage—seven years before Massachusetts would become the first to do so. Section 3, which *Windsor* struck down, had defined marriage as "a legal union between one man and one woman as husband and wife, and the word 'spouse' refers only to a person of the opposite sex who is a husband or a wife."

Justice Kennedy's opinion for the 5–4 majority pulled no punches. The "purpose and effect" of DOMA, he wrote, is "to disparage and to injure those whom the State, by its marriage laws, sought to protect in personhood and dignity." The law thus violates the Fifth Amendment guarantee that individuals may not be deprived of their "liberty" without "due process of law." The "Constitution protects" gay couples' "moral and sexual choices," Justice Kennedy wrote, but "DOMA writes inequality into the entire United States Code." Edith Windsor was saddled with a $363,053 estate tax bill when Clara Spyer, her romantic partner of nearly five decades (and spouse since 2007), died, but she would not have paid a cent on the inheritance if the federal government had recognized the couple's marriage. In addition to the estate tax, Justice Kennedy pointed to "over 1,000 statutes and numerous federal regulations," including "Social Security, housing, taxes, criminal sanctions, copyright, and veterans' benefits," that DOMA strips from gay and lesbian couples who are "unmarried for the purpose of federal law." The harms extend to emotional injury, Justice Kennedy wrote. DOMA permits gays and lesbians to enjoy only a "second-tier marriage" that "humiliates tens of thousands of children now being raised by same-sex couples."

In one of the most ironically influential dissenting opinions in the history of the Supreme Court, Justice Scalia lashed out at the majority for gutting DOMA with "legalistic argle-bargle." And he wrote this: "By formally declaring anyone opposed to same-sex marriage an enemy of human decency, the majority arms well every challenger to a state law restricting marriage to its traditional definition . . . As far as this Court is concerned, no one should be fooled: it is just a matter of listening and waiting for the other shoe."

The other shoe dropped more quickly than anyone—even Justice Scalia—could have imagined. Kennedy's majority opinion could have been interpreted less expansively, but thanks to the spin in Justice Scalia's vituperative dissent, the lower courts used it as an invitation to invalidate state bans on gay marriage. Only twelve months after *Windsor* came down on June 26, 2013, the Fourth Circuit court of appeals struck down bans in Maryland, North Carolina, South Carolina, and West Virginia. Three similar rulings followed over the next few months, knocking down same-sex marriage bans like a series of dominos. Many of the decisions quoted from Justice Scalia's dissent, using his words to bring about a result that is diametrically opposed to his jurisprudential and ideological position. And by the end of 2014, same-sex marriage was legal in thirty-seven states and the District of Columbia. Yet the Supreme Court demurred when asked to step into the fray in October 2014, denying certiorari in seven separate state attempts to reinstate their gay marriage bans. It took a ruling from Judge Jeffrey Sutton at the Sixth Circuit in November to finally push the justices to act. On January 16, 2015, the justices granted certiorari in four petitions out of four states (Kentucky, Michigan, Ohio, and Tennessee) challenging the Sixth Circuit decision.

Three months later, the parties' briefs, as well as amicus curiae ("friend of the court") briefs, came flying in. A modern record may have been set with a total of 147 amicus briefs—76 for petitioners, 66 for the respondents, and 5 more advocating neither side but generally agreeing that the gay marriage bans should be upheld. The little pamphlets, stacked up neatly in two piles in the Supreme Court's Public Information Office, measured more than two feet high.

It was a remarkably altered terrain in which the justices heard arguments on April 28, 2015. Popular support for same-sex marriage had doubled in fewer than two decades (from 27 percent in 1996 to 55 percent in 2015); two-thirds of Americans lived in places where gay marriage was legal; and nearly four hundred thousand gay and lesbian couples had exchanged vows. The court heard argument on two questions: First, is there a constitutional right, under the Fourteenth Amendment, for two people of the same sex to marry? Second, must states that do not allow same-sex couples to wed recognize valid, legally performed same-sex weddings in other states? It was a uniquely long hearing: ninety minutes were devoted to the first question and sixty to the second question.

The first and main round matched John Bursch, a former solicitor general for Michigan, against Mary Bonauto, the veteran gay-rights litigator once likened by Barney Frank, the former congressman from Massachusetts, to Thurgood Marshall. US Solicitor General Donald Verrilli also argued for the plaintiffs. Bonauto and Verrilli had the better day, but the session opened with signs that may have been discouraging to advocates of marriage equality.

During Bonauto's turn at the podium, several justices fretted over the prospect of upending a conception of marriage that has been around for "millennia." Chief Justice Roberts said no dictionary "prior to about a dozen years ago" fathoms marriage as anything but a "unity between a man and a woman as husband and wife." The gay couples in the lawsuits are "not seeking to join the institution," he said, but want "to change what the institution is." Justice Kennedy, the author of *Windsor* and two previous landmark opinions expanding gay rights, hinted that he wasn't a lock to do so again. "It's very difficult for the court to say, 'oh, well, we know better,'" he said.

One of the liberal justices, Stephen Breyer, wondered why "suddenly you want nine people outside the ballot box to require states that don't want to do it . . . to include gay people." Might it be wiser, he asked Bonauto, to "wait and see whether [same-sex marriage] is or is not harmful to marriage?" The best answer came later from Verrilli: "Gay and lesbian couples live openly as our neighbors . . . raise their children side by side with the rest of us, [and] contribute fully as members of the community." It is "simply untenable," he said, that "they can be required to wait" for equality. "They deserve it now."

The liberal justices came alive when Bursch took the lectern, impatient with his speculative contention that changing the definition of wedlock would bring undesirable consequences for society. Were marriage to be opened to same-sex couples, Bursch argued, the institution's central purpose—procreation and child-rearing— would take a severe hit. Children growing up with the idea that marriage is about "keeping that couple bound to that child forever" will be happier and more secure than children whose parents tied the knot merely because they have an "emotional commitment to each other," he said. "Ideas matter, Your Honors."

This line of attack withered under questioning. "You're not taking anything away from heterosexual couples" when the institution is opened to gays, Justice Ginsburg told Bursch. Justice Breyer observed that many gay couples are parents, while "a very high percent" of heterosexual couples do not or cannot procreate. For Justice Kagan, "it's hard to see how permitting same-sex marriage discourages people from being bonded with their biological children." Justice Sotomayor asked why a "feeling, which doesn't make any logical sense," should "control our decision making." Promisingly for supporters of same-sex marriage, Justice Kennedy criticized Bursch's argument that "only opposite-sex couples can have a bonding with the child." That, he said, is "just a wrong premise." And marriage is not just about raising children, Justice Kennedy reminded the lawyer for Michigan. Same-sex couples share the "more noble purpose" of marriage and the "dignity" that accompanies it whether or not they choose to become parents.

Without what Justice Breyer described as any "empirical connection" between same-sex marriage and tangible social harms, Bursch reverted near the end of the hearing to an argument about the democratic process and the role of the courts that would, two months later, fuel the dissenting opinions. "When you enact social change of this magnitude through the federal courts," he said, "it's cutting off . . . dialogue." It would be better, he urged, to "sit down and civilly discuss an issue and try to persuade each other through reason, love, and logic."

Perhaps the best early indication that a decision favorable to gay and lesbian couples was on its way was the listless second half of the hearing. After the fireworks during the first ninety minutes—which included an impressively voluble protestor who shouted of the "abomination" of gay marriage before he was removed from the courtroom— the justices seemed a little deflated and almost uninterested in the recognition question. The second session even ended ten minutes early.

When the decision in *Obergefell* arrived on June 26, it was no great surprise that marriage equality had prevailed or that Justice Kennedy had authored the majority opinion. The news was, nevertheless, stunning. And in contrast to two comparable landmark cases in the fight for equal rights for African Americans—*Brown v. Board of Education* in 1954 and *Loving v. Virginia* in 1967, both of which were decided unanimously—this win for gays and lesbians came with sixty-three pages of blistering and repetitive dissenting opinions attached. Each of the four dissenters—Chief Justice Roberts and Justices Samuel Alito, Antonin Scalia, and Clarence Thomas—wrote separately to emphasize the depth of their opposition to the idea of a constitutional right to gay marriage.

The majority opinion, joined by the four liberal justices, began with a sketch of the rise of gay rights over the past few decades and a sympathetic review of some of the "fourteen same-sex couples and two men whose same-sex partners are deceased." James Obergefell is one of these bereaved men. His husband, John Arthur, died of ALS in 2013 shortly after the two married on a tarmac in Maryland. (Arthur was too weak to leave the medically equipped plane.) But their home state of Ohio, where a ban on same-sex marriage was in place, refused to list Obergefell as Arthur's surviving spouse on the death certificate. These and thousands of other couples, Justice Kennedy wrote, "endure a substantial burden . . . Their stories reveal that they seek not to denigrate marriage but rather to live their lives, or honor their spouses' memory, joined by its bond."

Justice Kennedy's legal reasoning toward his conclusion that the Constitution requires states to open marriage to gays and lesbians was, for some, a bit spongy. He relied on neither a detailed assessment of "fundamental rights" under the Fourteenth Amendment's due process clause nor a deep inquiry into the contours of the same amendment's equal protection clause, the textual hook urged by the solicitor general. Instead, Justice Kennedy's opinion tracked the holistic appeal of Bonauto's opening line in the oral argument: "The intimate and committed relationships of same-sex couples, just like those of heterosexual couples, provide mutual support and are the foundation of family life in our society . . . [T]he stain of unworthiness that follows on individuals and families contravenes the basic constitutional commitment to equal dignity." The words "equal dignity" had first appeared in

Justice Kennedy's *Windsor* opinion and were echoed in the final lines of his *Obergefell* ruling:

> No union is more profound than marriage, for it embodies the highest ideals of love, fidelity, devotion, sacrifice, and family. In forming a marital union, two people become something greater than once they were. As some of the petitioners in these cases demonstrate, marriage embodies a love that may endure even past death. It would misunderstand these men and women to say they disrespect the idea of marriage. Their plea is that they do respect it, respect it so deeply that they seek to find its fulfillment for themselves. Their hope is not to be condemned to live in loneliness, excluded from one of civilization's oldest institutions. They ask for equal dignity in the eyes of the law. The Constitution grants them that right.

In his dissent, Chief Justice Roberts extended a hand to same-sex marriage supporters. "Many people will rejoice at this decision," he acknowledged, "and I begrudge none their celebration." But he was less gracious toward the five justices in the majority. "Five lawyers have closed the debate and enacted their own vision of marriage as a matter of constitutional law," he wrote. "Stealing this issue from the people will for many cast a cloud over same-sex marriage, making a dramatic social change that much more difficult to accept." While there may be "strong arguments rooted in social policy and considerations of fairness" for opening marriage laws to gays and lesbians, "this Court is not a legislature." The merits of same-sex marriage "should be of no concern to us. Under the Constitution, judges have power to say what the law is, not what it should be." He wrote that *Obergefell* is as unfounded as the court's "discredited" decision in *Lochner v. New York,* a 1905 ruling striking down a worker-protection bill based on a purported "liberty of contract" in the due process clause.

The other three dissenting justices made the court-as-usurper-of-democracy point repeatedly and even more bitingly. Justice Alito detected in the majority opinion a "deep and perhaps irremediable corruption of our legal culture's conception of constitutional interpretation." Justice Thomas added that *Obergefell* "rejects the idea—captured in our Declaration of Independence—that human dignity is innate and suggests instead that it comes from the Government." And most colorfully of all, Justice Scalia compared the majority opinion to "the aphorisms of a fortune cookie." The majority's "decree says that my Ruler, and the Ruler of 320 million Americans coast-to-coast, is a majority of the nine lawyers on the Supreme Court."

But this critique of the role of the court as tyrannical is all the dissenters had to offer. None of the justices spent time explaining the logic behind bans on same-sex marriage. All the chief justice could muster was this formalistic (and rather circular) logic, quoting Justice Sandra Day O'Connor's concurrence in *Lawrence v. Texas,* the 2003 case overturning a 1986 decision that had upheld state bans on homosexual sodomy: "[T]he marriage laws at issue here do not violate the equal protection clause, because distinguishing between opposite-sex and same-sex couples is rationally related to the States' 'legitimate state interest' in 'preserving the traditional institution of marriage.'"

What does that purported interest amount to? No justice summoned the outdated argument that homosexuality is beyond the moral pale. No justice suggested that gays and lesbians make bad parents. No justice picked up John Bursch's labored speculation in the oral argument that children might grow up worried that their parents are married only because they love each other. No dissenter *tried* to articulate a coherent explanation of why restricting marriage to its traditional definition is a "legitimate state interest." So after digesting the four dissents, a reader comes away with no reason to believe that anyone— not the couples themselves, not their potential children, not the wider society—suffers in any way from widened marriage rights.

Perhaps recognizing this, the chief justice returned near the end of his dissent to the *Lochner* bogeyman. Just as the *Obergefell* majority write that opening marriage to same-sex couples "pose[s] no risk of harm to themselves or third parties," Roberts wrote, *Lochner* "relied on its assessment that 'we think that a law like the one before us involves neither the safety, the morals nor the welfare of the public, and that the interest of the public is not in the slightest degree affected by such an act.'" But this comparison is deeply faulty. The Progressive Era reforms that were struck down in *Lochner* targeted unsafe and unhealthy working conditions. They did, in fact, prevent significant, tangible, and irreparable harm to others. Marriage equality bans, by all accounts, do nothing of the sort.

The struggle over gay rights is not at an end. About a third of Americans remain opposed to the liberalization of marriage laws mandated by the *Obergefell* ruling. Roy Moore, the chief justice of Alabama who defied earlier court rulings bringing gay marriage to his state, suggested that the Supreme Court was under the influence of Satan when it overturned the state bans. The Republican attorney general of Texas, Ken Paxton, condemned the court for what he called "lawlessness" and released county clerks from the duty of issuing marriage licenses to same-sex couples. If gay couples were to sue the clerks, he said, "numerous lawyers stand ready to assist clerks defending their religious beliefs."

And there is still no federal protection for gays and lesbians against discrimination in the workplace. Since Justice Kennedy's rationale was focused squarely on the right to marry and did not name gays and lesbians as a "suspect class" deserving special judicial solicitude under the equal protection clause, it does not provide direct support for arguments that other forms of differential treatment are unconstitutional. But as Gary Buseck, legal director of GLAD (Gay and Lesbian Advocates and Defenders) pointed out to me, the *Obergefell* opinion "effectively establish[ed]" that sexual orientation satisfies the four characteristics usually associated with a suspect class: (1) a discrete and insular minority that has suffered from (2) a history of discrimination and (3) political powerlessness based on (4) an immutable characteristic. So according to Buseck, *Obergefell* contains the seeds of a case for heightened scrutiny of other forms of discrimination against gays. But as of now, this protected status is inchoate rather than established. There are no legislative protections, either: a bill that would prevent employers from disfavoring gays, the Employment Non-Discrimination Act, has languished in Congress for more than twenty years, and a more comprehensive bill introduced in

July 2015, the Equality Act, faces steep resistance. In most states, a person marrying someone of the same sex could return from his honeymoon to find a pink slip from his homophobic boss—and have no legal recourse. "Now that same-sex couples can marry," Bonauto told me, "more people will come out on the job—with a desktop picture of their spouse, or when seeking a family policy of health insurance, or even by inviting their coworkers to the wedding—and there will inevitably be more discriminatory treatment."

A ruling on July 16, 2015, from the Equal Employment Opportunity Commission (EEOC) sets the stage for the next legal battle over gay rights that could reach the Supreme Court. By a vote of 3–2, the federal body charged with enforcing workplace rules decided that job discrimination against gays and lesbians is already illegal under Title VII of the Civil Rights Act of 1964. Title VII prohibits sex discrimination, the EEOC reasons, and mistreatment of gays and lesbians is a form of discrimination on the basis of sex. If "an employer suspends a lesbian employee for displaying a photo of her female spouse or her desk, but does not suspend a male employee for displaying a photo of his female spouse on his desk," the ruling reads, "[t]he lesbian employee . . . can allege that her employer took an adverse action against her that the employer would not have taken had she been male."

The EEOC is an agency, not a court, but courts generally "owe deference to the agency's expertise," says Bonauto. Still, some federal judges may refuse to accept the EEOC's logic, and this could lead to a circuit split on whether Title VII offers protections to gay and lesbian workers. That could bring the next Supreme Court battle over gay rights. Another question moving forward will be whether bakers, wedding photographers, and other small business owners who have a religious objection to gay marriage have a legal duty to do business with same-sex couples. This dilemma will occupy the public debate, and possibly further Supreme Court litigation, in the years to come. But October Term 2014 will go down in history for opening the institution of marriage to gay and lesbian Americans. It likely won't take long for the four *Obergefell* dissenters to be regarded with puzzlement for their ill-tempered resistance to the nation's inexorable march toward equality.

Epilogue

**Four Cases to Watch
in October Term 2015**

As of early August 2015, when this book went to press, the Supreme Court had agreed to hear thirty-five cases in the term beginning Monday, October 5, 2015. That's nearly half of the court's expected docket for the year and nine more cases than the justices had agreed to consider at the same point last year. The justices will likely add a handful of cases to their agenda following the so-called Long Conference on September 28, 2015. This is the catch-up meeting in which the justices consider dozens of petitions for certiorari that pile up in their chambers over the summer.

After a historic October Term 2014, it appears there will be no lull in the drama. Affirmative action in higher education; the fate of public-sector unions; the principle of one person, one vote; and at least four death-penalty cases are already teed up.

It is highly likely that the lightning-rod issue of abortion will return to the justices' plate as well. Cases out of Texas and Mississippi challenge new regulations that have effectively shuttered most abortion clinics in those states. The question in these cases is whether the new state laws constitute "undue burdens" on a woman's right to choose an abortion, obstacles that the Supreme Court said were unconstitutional in the *Casey v. Planned Parenthood* decision in 1992. A more fundamental challenge to abortion rights may also reach the Supreme Court. Several states have passed severely restrictive abortion laws that are blatantly unconstitutional under *Roe v. Wade,* the 1973 decision that first provided women with the right to have an abortion before fetal viability. North Dakota's fetal-heartbeat law, which would have banned abortion as early as six weeks after conception, earned a quick smackdown from the district court and the Eighth Circuit Court of Appeals. But the appellate court's opinion included a remarkable section suggesting that "[g]ood reasons exist for the court to reevaluate its jurisprudence" in *Roe.* The Court has afforded "too little consideration," the Eighth Circuit said, to states' "substantial interest in potential life throughout pregnancy." The appellate court is basically begging the justices to step in and dial back—or overturn—*Roe.*

Abortion will likely be a headlining issue in June 2016, when the justices issue their most controversial rulings. But other significant questions loom as well. Here is a preview of four important cases the justices have already agreed to take up during October Term 2015:

Montgomery v. Louisiana (Juvenile Criminal Justice)

Over the past decade, the Supreme Court has issued a trio of rulings curtailing punishments that may be imposed on juveniles. In 2005, the justices held in *Roper v. Simmons* that since offenders under the age of eighteen are more liable to peer pressure and bursts of impulsivity, they are less culpable than adults. Capital punishment for children thus constitutes cruel and unusual punishment in violation of the Eighth Amendment, the court decided. Five years later, similar reasoning motivated *Graham v. Florida*, a decision banning life sentences without the possibility of parole for young offenders who had committed crimes short of homicide. Both *Roper* and *Graham* were decided by votes of 6–3. A third case, *Miller v. Alabama*, produced a 5–4 split in 2012. The majority held that a mandatory sentence of life imprisonment for murder was unconstitutional as applied to criminals who had not reached their eighteenth birthday. In line with *Graham* and *Miller*, no one committing a crime before turning eighteen has been sentenced to life in prison over the past three years. But many prisoners in the United States who were sentenced before those decisions came down are today serving life terms for crimes they committed in their teenage years. In *Montgomery v. Louisiana*, the justices will decide whether the principle articulated in *Miller* applies retroactively to these offenders. If the court answers that question in the affirmative, some 1,500 prisoners will be resentenced to shorter terms and may taste freedom before they die.

Fisher v. University of Texas at Austin (Affirmative Action)

Affirmative action in higher education was found be constitutional in 1978, when a plurality of the justices decided, in *Regents of the University of California v. Bakke,* that using race as a "plus factor" in admissions comported with the equal protection clause. The Constitution prohibits the use of racial quotas, Justice Lewis Powell wrote, but a compelling state interest in diverse learning environments means that universities may consider race as one of many relevant factors in an individualized review of each applicant's file. The heart of *Bakke* was upheld in a pair of rulings involving admissions at the University of Michigan in 2003. While the undergraduate admissions policy assigning a given number of points to students based on their race was unconstitutional, the court held in *Gratz v. Bollinger,* the law school's less rigid goal of admitting a "critical mass" of qualified minorities was, per *Grutter v. Bollinger,* permissible. Abigail Fisher, a white woman who was rejected from the University of Texas at Austin in 2008, earned her first date at the Supreme Court in 2012. The university's consideration of race in its admissions policy had unconstitutionally excluded her, she said. Rather than fully resolve her claim, the justices asked the appeals court to reconsider whether the university's policy was "narrowly tailored" toward the goal of student diversity or whether an "available, workable, race-neutral alternative" could stand in its place. After a thorough review, the Fifth Circuit Court of Appeals endorsed UT–Austin's admissions policy for a second time in 2014. This prompted Fisher to file another writ of certiorari at the Supreme Court, which the justices granted. Both *Bakke* and *Grutter* may be on the chopping block: at stake in the second round of *Fisher v. University of Texas at Austin* (*Fisher II,* for short) is the future of racial diversity in higher education.

Friedrichs v. California Teachers Association (Public Unionism)

The Supreme Court is not a policy-making institution. Rather than seek out preferred constitutional questions, it sits passively, awaiting conflicts to come to it. But justices sometimes send not-so-subtle signals to potential litigants that they should bring a case their way. Such was the situation in 2014, when Justice Alito, in *Harris v. Quinn,* all but rolled out the red carpet for plaintiffs to challenge the court's 1977 ruling in *Abood v. Detroit Board of Education.* In *Abood,* the Supreme Court said that public-sector unions could collect an "agency fee" from public employees opting not to join the union. Teachers, police officers, and other public employees benefit from city contracts reached through collective bargaining, the court reasoned, so they may be compelled to pay these fees without violating their First Amendment right to free expression. Last year in *Harris,* Justice Alito called the reasoning in *Abood* "questionable" and noted that in previous decisions the court had considered it an "anomaly." He suggested that public employees' right to freedom of speech was weightier than the risk they may "free ride" off of a union that is bargaining in their interest. Accepting Justice Alito's invitation, Michael Carvin of the Center for Individual Rights orchestrated a suit explicitly designed to overturn *Abood.* In *Friedrichs,* a number of public-school teachers in California say that the compulsory fees they pay to the teachers' union violate their free speech rights. If the Supreme Court agrees, the rapid decline of private-sector unions in the United States will likely accelerate in the public sector. Public unions are at serious risk.

Evenwel v. Abbott (Voting Rights)

Perhaps the most consequential case coming up in October Term 2015 involves the meaning of "one person, one vote," a constitutional principle fundamental to American democracy. As chapter 6 explains, the Constitution requires that voters in a state should have roughly equal influence when electing state legislators and members of the House of Representatives. In 1964, in *Reynolds v. Sims,* the court held that although it is a "practical impossibility" to ensure "an identical number" of people in each state district, there "must be substantial equality of population among the various districts so that the vote of a citizen is approximately equal in weight to that of any other citizen in the state." But the court has never clarified who counts in figuring a district's "population." This is the matter the justices will consider in *Evenwel v. Abbott,* a challenge to the way Texas drew its state legislative lines in 2013. Texas has 31 state senators representing a population of 25.1 million. In line with the basic procedure used in every other state, simple division led the legislature to conclude that each of the 31 districts needed to include roughly 810,000 people. Its map resulted in a fairly even distribution—well within the Supreme Court's guideline of plus-or-minus 10 percent. Two voters in Texas were unhappy with this allocation, however. Sue Evenwel and Edward Pfenninger object that their votes are diluted in influence because the districts where they vote have a disproportionate number of eligible voters, whereas other districts are home to substantial numbers of children, noncitizens, and felons—people who cannot vote but who are counted toward the district population total nevertheless. The formula for divvying up districts should factor in the voter population, they say, not the raw total population, to give voters fair representation across the state. Some scholars have pointed out that data on numbers of eligible voters are not available, making such a count impossible. There are partisan and racial overtones of the challenge: the plaintiffs are represented by the Project on Fair Representation, a conservative group, and the districts they deem too big for their britches are home to substantial numbers of Democratic-voting Latinos. Most fundamentally, there are serious questions of democratic theory at stake. Do legislators represent only voters or the full body of the people? Are legal immigrants, children, and mentally incapacitated people bereft of representation in the United States, owing to their lack of a right to vote? In taking up *Evenwel,* the justices will confront previously unexplored issues at the heart of American electoral democracy.

Appendix

*Biographies of Current
Justices of the Supreme Court*

All biographies are derived from the US Supreme Court website: http://www.supremecourt.gov/biographies.aspx.

Chief Justice

John G. Roberts Jr., chief justice of the United States, was born in Buffalo, New York, January 27, 1955. He married Jane Marie Sullivan in 1996 and they have two children—Josephine and John. He received an AB from Harvard College in 1976 and a JD from Harvard Law School in 1979. He served as a law clerk for Judge Henry J. Friendly of the US Court of Appeals for the Second Circuit from 1979 to 1980 and as a law clerk for then associate justice William H. Rehnquist of the US Supreme Court during the 1980 term. He was special assistant to the attorney general, US Department of Justice, from 1981 to 1982; associate counsel to President Ronald Reagan, White House Counsel's Office, from 1982 to 1986;

and principal deputy solicitor general, US Department of Justice, from 1989 to 1993. From 1986 to 1989 and 1993 to 2003, he practiced law in Washington, DC. He was appointed to the US Court of Appeals for the DC Circuit in 2003. President George W. Bush nominated him as chief justice of the United States, and he took his seat September 29, 2005.

Associate Justices

All justices are listed in descending order of seniority.

Antonin Scalia was born in Trenton, New Jersey, on March 11, 1936. He married Maureen McCarthy and has nine children—Ann Forrest, Eugene, John Francis, Catherine Elisabeth, Mary Clare, Paul David, Matthew, Christopher James, and Margaret Jane. He received his AB from Georgetown University and the University of Fribourg, Switzerland; received his LLB from Harvard Law School; and was a Sheldon Fellow of Harvard University from 1960 to 1961. He was in private practice in Cleveland, Ohio, from 1961 to 1967; a professor of law at the University of Virginia from 1967 to 1971; a professor of law at the University of Chicago from 1977 to 1982; and a visiting professor of law at Georgetown University and Stanford University. He was chairman of the American Bar Association's Section of Administrative Law, 1981–82, and its Conference of Section Chairmen, 1982–83. He served the federal government as general counsel for the Office of Telecommunications Policy from 1971 to 1972, chairman of the Administrative Conference of the United States from 1972 to 1974, and assistant attorney general for the Office of Legal Counsel from 1974 to 1977. He was appointed judge of the US Court of Appeals for the DC Circuit in 1982. President Ronald Reagan nominated him as an associate justice of the Supreme Court, and he took his seat September 26, 1986.

Anthony M. Kennedy was born in Sacramento, California, July 23, 1936. He married Mary Davis and has three children. He received his BA from Stanford University and the London School of Economics and his LLB from Harvard Law School. He was in private practice in San Francisco, California, from 1961 to 1963, as well as in Sacramento, California, from 1963 to 1975. From 1965 to 1988, he was a professor of constitutional law at the McGeorge School of Law, University of the Pacific. He has served in numerous positions during his career, including as a member of the California Army National Guard in 1961, the board of the Federal Judicial Center from 1987 to 1988, and two committees of the Judicial Conference of the United States: the Advisory Panel on Financial Disclosure Reports and Judicial Activities, subsequently renamed the Advisory Committee on Codes of Conduct, from 1979 to 1987, and the Committee on Pacific Territories from 1979 to 1990, which he chaired from 1982 to 1990. He was appointed to the US Court of Appeals for the Ninth Circuit in 1975. President Ronald Reagan nominated him as an associate justice of the Supreme Court, and he took his seat February 18, 1988.

Clarence Thomas was born in the Pin Point community of Georgia near Savannah June 23, 1948. He married Virginia Lamp in 1987 and has one child, Jamal Adeen, by a previous marriage. He attended Conception Seminary and received an AB cum laude from Holy Cross College and a JD from Yale Law School in 1974. He was admitted to law practice in Missouri in 1974 and served as an assistant attorney general of Missouri from 1974 to 1977, an attorney with the Monsanto Company from 1977 to 1979, and legislative assistant to Senator John Danforth from 1979 to 1981. From 1981 to 1982, he served as assistant secretary for civil rights, US Department of Education, and as chairman of the US Equal Employment Opportunity Commission from 1982 to 1990. He became a judge of the US Court of Appeals for the DC Circuit in 1990. President George H. W. Bush nominated him as an associate justice of the Supreme Court, and he took his seat October 23, 1991.

Ruth Bader Ginsburg was born in Brooklyn, New York, March 15, 1933. She married Martin D. Ginsburg in 1954, and has a daughter, Jane, and a son, James. She received her BA from Cornell University, attended Harvard Law School, and received her LLB from Columbia Law School. She served as a law clerk to the Honorable Edmund L. Palmieri, judge of the US District Court for the Southern District of New York, from 1959 to 1961. From 1961 to 1963, she was a research associate and then associate director of the Columbia Law School Project on International Procedure. She was a professor of law at Rutgers University School of Law from 1963 to 1972 and Columbia Law School from 1972 to 1980 and a fellow at the Center for

Advanced Study in the Behavioral Sciences in Stanford, California, from 1977 to 1978. In 1971, she was cofounder of the Women's Rights Project of the American Civil Liberties Union and served as the ACLU's general counsel from 1973 to 1980 and on the ACLU National Board of Directors from 1974 to 1980. She served on the board and executive committee of the American Bar Foundation from 1979 to 1989, on the board of editors of the *American Bar Association Journal* from 1972 to 1978, and on the Council of the American Law Institute from 1978 to 1993. She was appointed a judge of the US Court of Appeals for the DC Circuit in 1980. President Bill Clinton nominated her as an associate justice of the Supreme Court, and she took her seat August 10, 1993.

Stephen G. Breyer was born in San Francisco, California, August 15, 1938. He married Joanna Hare in 1967 and has three children—Chloe, Nell, and Michael. He received an AB from Stanford University; a BA from Magdalen College, Oxford; and an LLB from Harvard Law School. He served as a law clerk to Justice Arthur Goldberg of the US Supreme Court during the 1964 term; as a special assistant to the assistant US attorney general for antitrust, 1965–67; as an assistant special prosecutor of the Watergate Special Prosecution Force, 1973; as special counsel of the US Senate Judiciary Committee, 1974–75; and as chief counsel of the committee, 1979–80. He was an assistant professor, professor of law, and lecturer at Harvard Law School, 1967–94; a professor at the Harvard University Kennedy School of Government, 1977–80; and a visiting professor at the College of Law, Sydney,

Australia, and at the University of Rome. From 1980 to 1990, he served as a judge of the US Court of Appeals for the First Circuit and as its chief judge, 1990–94. He also served as a member of the Judicial Conference of the United States, 1990–1994, and the US Sentencing Commission, 1985–89. President Bill Clinton nominated him as an associate justice of the Supreme Court, and he took his seat August 3, 1994.

Samuel Anthony Alito Jr. was born in Trenton, New Jersey, April 1, 1950. He married Martha-Ann Bomgardner in 1985, and has two children—Philip and Laura. He served as a law clerk for Leonard I. Garth of the US Court of Appeals for the Third Circuit from 1976 to 1977. He was assistant US attorney, District of New Jersey, 1977–81; assistant to the solicitor general, US Department of Justice, 1981–85; deputy assistant attorney general, US Department of Justice, 1985–87; and US attorney, District of New Jersey, 1987–90. He was appointed to the US Court of Appeals for the Third Circuit in 1990. President George W. Bush nominated him as an associate justice of the Supreme Court, and he took his seat January 31, 2006.

Sonia Sotomayor was born in Bronx, New York, on June 25, 1954. She earned a BA in 1976 from Princeton University, graduating summa cum laude and receiving the university's highest academic honor. In 1979, she earned a JD from Yale Law School, where she served as an editor of the *Yale Law Journal*. She served as assistant district attorney in the New York County District Attorney's Office from 1979 to 1984. She then litigated international commercial matters in New York City at Pavia and Harcourt, where she served as an associate and then partner from 1984 to 1992. In 1991, President George H. W. Bush nominated her to the US District Court for the Southern District of New York, and she served in that role from 1992 to 1998. She served as a judge on the US Court of Appeals for the Second Circuit from 1998 to 2009. President Barack Obama nominated her as an associate justice of the Supreme Court on May 26, 2009, and she assumed this role August 8, 2009.

Elena Kagan was born in New York, New York, on April 28, 1960. She received an AB from Princeton University in 1981, an M Phil from Oxford in 1983, and a JD from Harvard Law School in 1986. She clerked for Judge Abner Mikva of the US Court of Appeals for the DC Circuit from 1986 to 1987 and for Justice Thurgood Marshall of the US Supreme Court during the 1987 term. After briefly practicing law at a Washington, DC, law firm, she became a law professor, first at the University of Chicago Law School and later at Harvard Law School. She also served for four years in the Clinton administration as associate counsel to the president and then as deputy assistant to the president for domestic policy. Between 2003 and 2009, she served as the dean of Harvard Law School. In 2009, President Barack Obama nominated her as the solicitor general of the United States. After serving in that role for a year, the president nominated her as an associate justice of the Supreme Court on May 10, 2010. She took her seat August 7, 2010.

Retired Justices

All justices are listed in order of retirement.

Sandra Day O'Connor, (retired) associate justice, was born in El Paso, Texas, March 26, 1930. She married John Jay O'Connor III in 1952 and has three sons—Scott, Brian, and Jay. She received her BA and LLB from Stanford University. She served as Deputy County Attorney of San Mateo County, California, from 1952 to 1953 and as a civilian attorney for Quartermaster Market Center, Frankfurt, Germany, from 1954 to 1957. From 1958 to 1960, she practiced law in Maryvale, Arizona, and served as assistant attorney general of Arizona from 1965 to 1969. She was appointed to the Arizona State Senate in 1969 and was subsequently reelected to two two-year terms. In 1975 she was elected judge of the Maricopa County Superior Court and served until 1979, when she was appointed to the Arizona Court of Appeals. President Ronald Reagan nominated her as an associate justice of the Supreme Court, and she took her seat September 25, 1981. Justice O'Connor retired from the Supreme Court on January 31, 2006.

David H. Souter, (retired) associate justice, was born in Melrose, Massachusetts, September 17, 1939. He graduated from Harvard College, from which he received his AB. After two years as a Rhodes Scholar at Magdalen College, Oxford, he received an AB in jurisprudence from Oxford University and an MA in 1989. After receiving an LLB from Harvard Law School, he was an associate at Orr and Reno in Concord, New Hampshire, from 1966 to 1968, when he became an assistant attorney general of New Hampshire. In 1971, he became deputy attorney general and, in 1976, attorney general of New Hampshire. In 1978, he was named an associate justice of the Superior Court of New Hampshire and was appointed to the Supreme Court of New Hampshire as an associate justice in 1983. He became a judge of the US Court of Appeals for the First Circuit on May 25, 1990. President George H. W. Bush nominated him as an associate justice of the Supreme Court, and he took his seat October 9, 1990. Justice Souter retired from the Supreme Court on June 29, 2009.

John Paul Stevens, (retired) associate justice, was born in Chicago, Illinois, April 20, 1920. He married Maryan Mulholland and has four children—John Joseph (deceased), Kathryn, Elizabeth Jane, and Susan Roberta. He received an AB from the University of Chicago and a JD from the Northwestern University School of Law. He served in the US Navy from 1942 to 1945 and was a law clerk to Justice Wiley Rutledge of the US Supreme Court during the 1947 term. He was admitted to law practice in Illinois in 1949. He was associate counsel to the Subcommittee on the Study of Monopoly Power of the Judiciary Committee of the US House of Representatives, 1951–52, and a member of the attorney general's National Committee to Study Antitrust Law, 1953–55. He was second vice president of the Chicago Bar Association in 1970. From 1970 to 1975, he served as a judge of the US Court of Appeals for the Seventh Circuit. President Gerald Ford nominated him as an associate justice of the Supreme Court, and he took his seat December 19, 1975. Justice Stevens retired from the Supreme Court on June 29, 2010.

CPSIA information can be obtained at www.ICGtesting.com
Printed in the USA
BVOW08*0745161115

426603BV00002BB/2/P